T0318410

Identity (Re)constructions After Brain Injury

Identity (Re)constructions After Brain Injury: Personal and Family Identity investigates how being diagnosed with acquired brain injury (ABI) impacts identity (re)construction in both adults with ABI and their close relatives.

To show how being diagnosed with ABI impacts identity (re)construction, this book investigates key patterns of identity construction. Discourse analysis, especially on the concept of positioning, provides an understanding of the changes and developmental processes in these self-narratives. These narrative (re)constructions point to a developmental change of identity in the course of the different phases of the recovery process for both persons with ABI and their relatives, including conflicting voices from society, service providers, relatives, and other adults with ABI. In addition, the (re)construction process is characterized by much ambivalence in both ABI survivors and relatives.

Three perspectives are triangulated: (1) an insider perspective from ABI survivors; (2) an insider perspective from relatives; and (3) an outsider perspective from the researchers. This allows us to see how identities are negotiated and constructed in concrete situations. This innovative book will be required reading for all students and academics working in the fields of disability studies, rehabilitation psychology, sociology, allied health, and social care.

Chalotte Glintborg, Ph.D. in psychology, is a scientist from Aalborg University who specialises in rehabilitation psychology. Her research has centred on exploring first person perspectives on the emotional consequences of living with disabilities, including identity problems, distress, shame, and depression.

Interdisciplinary Disability Studies

Series editor: Mark Sherry, The University of Toledo, USA

Disability studies has made great strides in exploring power and the body. This series extends the interdisciplinary dialogue between disability studies and other fields by asking how disability studies can influence a particular field. It will show how a deep engagement with disability studies changes our understanding of the following fields: sociology, literary studies, gender studies, bioethics, social work, law, education, or history. This ground-breaking series identifies both the practical and theoretical implications of such an interdisciplinary dialogue and challenges people in disability studies as well as other disciplinary fields to critically reflect on their professional praxis in terms of theory, practice, and methods.

For a full list of titles in this series, please visit www.routledge.com/series/ASHSER1401

Identity (Re)constructions After Brain Injury

Personal and Family Identity

Chalotte Glintborg

Routledge
Taylor & Francis Group

LONDON AND NEW YORK

First published 2019
by Routledge
2 Park Square, Milton Park, Abingdon, Oxon OX14 4RN

and by Routledge
605 Third Avenue, New York, NY 10017

First issued in paperback 2020

Routledge is an imprint of the Taylor & Francis Group, an informa business

British Library Cataloguing in Publication Data
A catalogue record for this book is available from the British Library

Library of Congress Cataloging-in-Publication Data
A catalog record has been requested for this book

ISBN 13: 978-0-367-72881-6 (pbk)
ISBN 13: 978-0-8153-9554-6 (hbk)

Typeset in Times New Roman
by Taylor & Francis Books

Contents

Illustrations

Figures

Table

List of co-authors

Co-authors for Chapter 11

Hana Malá Rytter, Ph.D. is Associate Professor in Neuropsychology at the Department of Psychology, University of Copenhagen, Denmark and at the Department of Neurology, Copenhagen University Hospital, Bispebjerg-Frederiksberg, Denmark, where she also serves a clinical role. Her research topics include approaches to improve the recovery of cognitive function after brain injury, brain plasticity, and rehabilitative environment.

Camilla Jørgensen is a clinical psychologist at the Center for Developmental and Applied Psychological Science, Department of Communication and Psychology, Aalborg University, Denmark. Her clinical work is in the field of supporting families who have a child with a disability.

Maria Natalie Ramskov Thomassen, is a clinical psychologist at the Center for Developmental and Applied Psychological Science, Department of Communication and Psychology, Aalborg University, Denmark. Her clinical work is in the field of supporting clients with disabilities to return to work.

Preface

Lillian wakes up at the neurorehabilitation center (NRC) after two weeks in a coma. She describes herself as being super happy to be alive and she is happy to see Lars (her husband) again. *"It is like we are falling in love all over again,"* she says. However, Lillian is told by a neuropsychologist that she seems almost artificially happy, and it is noted in her journal that they [the professionals] must be aware of behavioral changes. Lillian is amazed by this description in the journal, since she *really* felt happy to be alive at this point.

Lillian is discharged to another NRC. Lillian sticks to her professional identity and thinks that she has to continue her rehabilitation at work, but it does not turn out this way. At the NRC, a physiotherapist draws a staircase for Lillian with the developmental steps that could occur in her rehabilitation process. *"This staircase has been very helpful and illustrative to me,"* she says. Lillian also mentions that she came to the NRC in a wheelchair, but walked when she was discharged.

Lillian is discharged to her private home. Lillian describes the following period as turbulent, and she finds it difficult to accept the "new me," as she calls it. *"Not until this summer* [five years post-injury] *has the new Lillian landed,"* she says. *"It has taken me a long time to find ease with the 'new me,' but I'm finding ease with her now."* Lillian talks a lot about identity and says: *"I'm still working with the new Lillian – I'm not done discovering her,"* which she tells me five years after the brain injury occurred. She also tells me that she had to say goodbye properly to the old Lillian, and that it is important to be able to mourn about what could have happened. Lillian says that *"… everyone* [professionals] *can talk about injuries and symptoms, but not the deep personal things – there is a scariness, a lack of knowledge, and a lack of recognition of it as important."* Lillian is amazed about how little people talk about this both within the rehabilitation system, and outside it. *"We talk way too little about personal competences and working on developing them,"* she says.

Lillian also would have liked professionals to have talked to her about intimacy. *"It was us who had to bring it up and not the professionals who came to support me in my private home,"* she says. When Lillian was discharged, she and her husband tried to have sex. But Lillian found that she had difficulties in conducting intercourse with her husband. There were different issues with this, which no one had talked to her about. She remembers that there was a fellow patient at the rehabilitation center who asked for information, but he was only given a brochure. When Lillian later brought up the topic, she was met with a shyness from the professionals that came to support her in the house. Instead, she googled information and sought help from her private practitioner.

For Lars (her husband), being able to be with Lillian has been central. He visited her every day at both rehabilitation centers despite the two-hour drive. At the first rehabilitation center, Lars expressed concern that he lacked contact with the staff. There was no meeting when Lillian was first hospitalized and they were not invited to tell their story or talk about who they were. *"It was much better at the second rehabilitation center – there they showed interest in us as a couple,"* he says.

Lars experiences an emotional breakdown a while after Lillian has returned home. He had to reach out to his own private practitioner as none of the rehabilitation professionals who supported Lillian, were supporting Lars in his process. Lillian highlighted that she had been addressing Lars's condition during the discharge meeting at the rehabilitation center with some of the professionals, but they did not react to this information. Today, the couple denotes Lars's reaction as compassion fatigue, and emphasizes the importance of taking better care of relatives as part of the rehabilitation as well.

"As long as the injured person is very ill, the focus is there, but when things get more stable, the emotional strain on relatives becomes clear as well," Lars says. Lars was offered antidepressant medication by his doctor, but he said no to this. He had to deal with his experience in other ways.

Lillian says that after her brain injury she has become more sensitive and much more in touch with her values. Likewise, she says that she and her husband work hard to hold on to the feeling of normality, as all their focus can easily be drawn to the brain injury and disability.

This case study contains fictional names but is an actual case from my research. It presents issues that represent many of the included adults with acquired brain injury (ABI) and their close relatives. This case contextualizes the field in which my research is situated, with a special focus on psychosocial consequences. Furthermore, this preface illustrates inside perspectives and gives insight into how the same situation can be perceived and narrated quite differently from the perspectives of professionals, a first-person ABI survivor's perspective, and a relative's perspective. This preface serves as a starting point from where the process of identity (re)construction after ABI begins for adults with ABI and their relatives.

Part I

Theoretical frameworks and methods

The following chapters unfolds the state of art in identity research in ABI and what methods used in narrative inquiry. In addition, a chapter will cover some of the dilemmas met while doing data collection in the private homes of adults with ABI and their close relatives.

1   Introduction

Once a person is diagnosed with ABI, there is a risk that this label can actually become the overriding means of defining the identity not only of that person, but also of that person's whole family. Reification of the diagnosis of a brain injury can be oppressive, because it subjugates humanity in such a way that everything a person does can be interpreted as part of the neurological disability. This book sums up my research within the field of acquired brain injury (ABI) for the last six years, with a special focus on identity and identity (re)construction.

It started with my Ph.D. (Glintborg, 2015), which focused on coordination in ABI rehabilitation within a bio–psycho–social framework. More specifically, I investigated the effects of coordinated rehabilitation programs in Denmark. In addition, I also explored what helps or hinders positive rehabilitation outcomes, as seen from an ABI survivor's and their relatives' perspectives.

My research centers on three main areas: (1) development within brain injury rehabilitation, (2) the bio–psycho–social model as operationalized by the International Classification of Functioning (ICF), and (3) rehabilitation as seen from an ABI survivor's and their relatives' perspectives. Neuroscience has developed from seeing the brain as an organization of specialized modules to seeing it as a complex collaboration between different centers, with a capacity for change and relocation of functions (neuroplasticity). In addition, research has shown that bio–psycho–social aspects interact, e.g. emotional needs affect cognitive functions and vice versa (Cicerone & Fraser, 2000). Therefore, rehabilitation should be based on a comprehensive bio–psycho–social approach. The United Nations (UN) and the World Health Organization (WHO) recommend rehabilitation based on a multidisciplinary, coherent approach. The UN Convention on the Rights of Persons with Disabilities, Article

26, describes the requirements for habilitation and rehabilitation as follows: "Services and programs begin at the earliest possible stage and are based on the multidisciplinary assessment of individuals' needs and strengths ..." (United Nations, 2006). The WHO defines rehabilitation as follows:

> Rehabilitation of people with disabilities is a process aimed at enabling them to reach and maintain their optimal physical, sensory, intellectual, psychological and social functional levels. Rehabilitation provides disabled people with the tools they need to attain independence and self-determination.
>
> (WHO, 2011)

Furthermore, the WHO recommends the ICF (the bio–psycho–social model) as a framework for disabilities. After ABI, the psychosocial aspects of recovery are known to be a particular challenge in rehabilitation practice (Morton & Wehmann, 1995; Teasdale & Engberg, 2004; 2005). Therefore, my research specifically focuses on the psychosocial outcomes of rehabilitation programs. In my Ph.D. and my postdoctoral follow-up study, I used a prospective, naturalistic, mixed-methods design to investigate bio–psycho–social recovery outcomes and perceptions of the rehabilitation programs. The empirical data was derived from 82 adults aged 18–66 years with a moderate or severe ABI and 40 of their relatives. Quantitative data were gathered from psychometric tests (Functional Independence Measure, FIM; Major Depression Inventory, MDI; WHO Quality of Life, WHOQOL (BREF); Impact on Participation and Autonomy Questionnaire, IPAQ), as well as information on return to work. The qualitative study was based on interviews with persons with ABI and their relatives about factors they see as important for recovery.

For further reading, the results of the Ph.D. were reported in four empirical articles (Glintborg & Jensen de López, 2014; Glintborg, 2015; Glintborg & Hansen, 2016; Glintborg, Thomsen, & Hansen, 2018). In summary, my research concluded that coordinated rehabilitation programs did not influence bio–psycho–social outcomes. The tests revealed that ABI survivors experienced the same level of difficulties after receiving support from the new program as the group that underwent the standard rehabilitation. The total FIM scores for persons with ABI were above the cut-off for independence at discharge from the rehabilitation center and remained stable at follow-up. With regard to psychosocial outcomes, one-third of all clients showed signs of depression and more than half (60 percent) of all clients experienced dissatisfaction with physical, environmental, and psychological quality of life (QOL). Furthermore, 50 percent of all clients reported problems in their family relationships. These bio–psycho–social outcome levels resonate with levels found in other studies (e.g. Morton & Vehman, 1995; Hall, Mann, High, Kreutzer, & Wood, 1996; Jorge et al., 1993; Jorge et al., 2004; Teasdale & Engberg, 2004; 2005; Hackett & Anderson, 2005; Brenner & Homaifar, 2009). However, the qualitative study revealed some of the factors that might improve rehabilitation outcomes (see Glintborg, Thomsen, & Hansen, 2018).

Identity loss after ABI was revealed as a dominant theme across all 82 persons with ABI at one-year follow-up. The analysis revealed a developmental change of identity in the course of the different phases of the rehabilitation and recovery process. Furthermore, conflicting voices were identified from society, service providers, relatives, and the adults with ABI themselves. In addition, the reconstruction process was characterized by much ambivalence. These results were discussed in the light of current identity research in Glintborg (2015). The use of a narrative approach in rehabilitation was suggested in order to help individuals transform into new narrative identities. After the Ph.D., I had the opportunity to follow the participants who took part in my Ph.D. research in a longitudinal study (five-year follow-up). The qualitative part of my Ph.D. and the five-year follow-up form the empirical grounding of this book with a special focus on identity and identity (re)construction in adults with ABI and families up to five years post-injury. In addition, three colleagues and I carried out a study of the role of peer support groups in identity (re)construction, which is also included in this book (see Chapter 11). The aims of the study were to expand our current knowledge of peer support groups for individuals with ABI and to contribute to our understanding of how the process of identity (re)construction is influenced by participation in such a group.

Thus, this book highlights how being diagnosed with ABI impacts identity (re)construction after ABI in both adults with ABI and their close relatives. Throughout the book, three perspectives are explored – (1) an insider perspective from ABI survivors; (2) an insider perspective from relatives; and (3) an outside perspective from researchers – in order to illustrate how identities are negotiated, and constructed in concrete situations.

This book describes key patterns of identity construction found in this research. It unfolds reconstructions of identity through self-narratives by appeal to methods of discourse analysis, drawing especially on the concept of positioning, and placing particular focus on changes and developmental processes in these self-narratives.

References

Brenner, L. A. & Homaifar, B. Y. (2009). Development-acquired TBI and suicidality: Risk and assessment. In L. Sher & A. Vilens (Eds.). *War and suicide* (pp. 189–202). Hauppauge, NY: Nova Science Publishers.

Cicerone, K. D. & Fraser, R. T. (2000). Counselling interactions for clients with traumatic brain injury. In R. T. Fraser & D. Clemmons (Eds.). *Traumatic brain injury rehabilitation: Practical vocational, neuropsychological, and psychotherapy interventions* (pp. 95–127). Boca Raton, FL: CRC Press.

Glintborg, C. (2015). *Grib mennesket. En konceptuel og empirisk undersøgelse af koordineret rehabilitering: objektivt bio-psyko-social udbytte for voksne med erhvervet hjerneskade samt klienters og pårørendes oplevelse af rehabiliteringen med og uden kommunal coordination* [Seize the self! An empirical mixed methods study of the bio–psycho–social recovery outcomes and perceptions of a coordinated neurorehabilitation program]. Ph.D. thesis, The Faculty of Humanities. Aalborg, Denmark: Aalborg University. Available at: http://www. hcci.aau.dk/digitalAssets/129/129472_chalotte_glintborg_phd-afhandling.pdf.

Glintborg, C. & Hansen, T. (2016). Bio–psyko–social effects of a coordinated neurorehabilitation program: A naturalistic mixed methods study. *NeuroRehabilitation*, 38(2), 99–113.

Glintborg, C. & Jensen de López, K. (2014). Koordination i et nyt lys – sikring af de psykologiske indsatser i hjerneskaderehabiliteringen [Coordination in a new light – ensuring the psychological efforts in brain injury rehabilitation]. *Psyke & Logos*, 34(2), 228–246.

Glintborg, C., Thomsen, A., & Hansen, T. (2018). Beyond broken bodies and brains: A mixed methods study of mental health and life transitions after brain injury. *Brain Impairment*, 19(3), 215–227.

Hackett, M. L. & Anderson, C. S. (2005). Predictors of depression after stroke. A systematic review of observational studies. *Stroke*, 36(10), 2296–2301.

Hall, K. M., Mann, N., High, W. M., Kreutzer, J. S., & Wood, D. (1996). Functional measures after traumatic brain injury: Ceiling effects of FIM, FIM +FAM, DRS and CIQ. *Journal of Head Trauma Rehabilitation*, 11(5), 27–39.

Jorge, R. E., Robinson, R. G., Arndt, S. V., Starkstein, S. E., Forrester, A. W., & Geisler, F. (1993). Depression following traumatic brain injury: a 1 year longitudinal study. *Journal of Affective Disorders*, 27(4), 233–243.

Jorge, R. E., Robinson, R. G., Moser, D., Tateno, A., Crespo-Facorro, B., & Arndt, S. V. (2004). Major depression following traumatic brain injury. *Archives of General Psychiatry*, 61(1), 42–50.

Morton, M. V. & Wehman, P. (1995). Psychosocial and emotional sequelae of individuals with traumatic brain injury: A literature review and recommendations. *Brain Injury*, 9(1), 81–92.

WHO (2011). *World Report on Disability*. [online] World Health Organization. Available at: https://www.who.int/disabilities/world_report/2011/report.pdf.

Teasdale, T. W. & Engberg, A. W. (2004). Psychosocial outcome following traumatic brain injury in adults: A long-term population-based follow up. *Brain Injury*, 18(6), 535–545.

Teasdale, T. W. & Engberg, A. W. (2005). Psychosocial consequences of stroke: A long-term population-based follow-up. *Brain Injury*, 19(12), 1049–1058.

United Nations (2006). *International convention on the rights of people with disabilities*. [online] United Nations Official Website. Available at: http://www.un.org/disabilities/convention/conventionfull.shtml.

2 Self-identity in people with acquired brain injury

Research in self-identity after acquired brain injury was addressed in a keynote speech by Professor Barbara Wilson in 2010 as one of the top ten cutting-edge developments in the field of neurorehabilitation. It is crucial to understand the means and interplay between brain systems, cognition, and personal and social identity. Based on this, Ownsworth wrote the first book dedicated to self-identity issues after brain injury (Ownsworth, 2014). In comparison to psychological adjustment after brain injury (e.g. coping), the literature focusing specifically on identity and identity reconstruction after ABI is relatively sparse. However, there is a growing body of studies demonstrating the negative impact of ABI on identity (e.g. Nochi, 1998; Gracey, Evan, & Malley, 2008; Glintborg, 2016). A meta-synthesis by Levack, Kayes, and Fadyl (2010) of 23 qualitative studies found that six of the eight major themes regarding experiences with brain injury were related to disconnection with self (compared to pre-injury self) and reconstructing identity, place in the world, and personhood. This disconnection was attributed to complex changes in functioning and life situation. A more recent review by Beadle, Ownsworth, Fleming, and Shum (2016) of 15 studies also provided evidence of mostly negative changes to self-concept. Changes in physical appearance have also been found to contribute to poor self-concept after ABI due to perceived or actual negative reactions from the public (e.g. Morris et al., 2005). A study by Jumisko, Lexell, and Soderberg (2005) found that people with traumatic brain injuries described their body as "an enemy" due to physical symptoms (e.g. fatigue, pain, etc.). Thus, the impact of physical impairment and loss of mobility on the sense of self has received the most attention in the ABI literature.

A study by Ownsworth, Fleming, Strong, Radel, Chan, and Clare (2007) found that, although awareness deficits and executive impairment may not preclude functional gains, individuals with these characteristics might not experience the same degree of psychosocial recovery as individuals with good awareness. Thus, individuals with neuropsychologicallybased awareness deficits could potentially benefit from early intervention to enhance their psychosocial adjustment.

However, memory impairment has also received considerable attention in the literature. The subjective experience of people suffering from amnesia was explored by Nochi (1997; 1998) who referred to blank periods of memory loss as a void, which disrupted adults' understanding of past and present and threatened their sense of agency. Cloute, Mitches, and Yates (2008) also investigated memory problems and how they affected people's ability to offer personal accounts, thus contributing to passive positioning within the medical system and society.

The issue of how communication impairment impacts self-identity has received considerable attention in research, investigating adjustment to aphasia (Shadden, 2005; Shadden & Koski, 2007; Silverman, 2011). Renegotiation of identity in circumstances of aphasia depends on how the affected person and their close relatives adapt to communication difficulties (Shadden, 2005).

Some of the most distressing changes to self after ABI include social perception and emotion regulation deficits, i.e. loss of empathy, loss of perspective-taking skills, lack of emotional responsiveness, reduced tolerance to stress, and poor anger control (Ownsworth, 2014). Jumisko, Lexell, and Soderberg (2005) identified that people with a traumatic brain injury (TBI) had a sense that they had "lost something of themselves." It was observed that they had difficulties understanding their own feelings and reading the emotions of others. In sum, the changes to physical, cognitive, and socio-emotional functions after ABI can alter the experience of the self (Gracey et al., 2008).

The broader research on self-identity after ABI has mainly focused on self-concept or self-esteem, rather than self-identity and how identity is (re)constructed after ABI. In addition, accounts from ABI survivors themselves have not been seen as reliable or as important sources of information (Gracey et al., 2008). Consequently, outcome measures alone, such as scores on depression and anxiety indices, have been thought to be indicators of rehabilitation progress (Johnson, Goverover, & Dijkers, 2005). And thus, most studies about ABI and the self have approached the topic from a medical or neuropsychological point of view. How individuals construct and co-construct themselves has rarely been valued. However, as pointed out by Moldover et al. (2004): "(ABI) is not only a neuropathological event but also a unique psychological process with profound implications for identity development" (p. 151).

ABI is not only a pathological matter but it also triggers a process of identity development. This process includes a grieving process (saying goodbye to the old self) and a process of reconstructing a new identity.

Consequently, Cantor and colleagues argue that a person with ABI lives with two images of self: *"who I am now"* and *"who I was before"* (Cantor et al., 2005, p. 531). When suffering from a brain injury, a person's sense of coherence is therefore challenged. That is, the predictability of usual life is suddenly lost – and with references to Ellis-Hill's Life Thread Model, the life threads are broken and frayed (Ellis-Hill, Payne, & Ward, 2008). The many threads in the model represent the variety of stories we can tell about ourselves. These stories are created between people (a teller and audience). In this way, the Life Thread Model suggests that rehabilitation processes are not only physical but that discursive psychological and social processes are also involved. As found in a study by Carpenter (1994), long-term survivors of spinal cord injuries, who defined themselves as having successfully adapted, had not improved physically over time but had redefined themselves.

Not only do ABI survivors deal with broken life threads and a pre- and post-identity, but the same can also be said for their relatives. Balancing these identity dilemmas can be stressful, and can have psychological consequences for both ABI survivors and relatives. Therefore, a brain injury should not only be seen as a neurological trauma, but also as a psychological trauma that impacts a person's whole life as well as the lives of their relatives. However, hardly any studies have focused on the relatives' identity (re)construction after ABI, or how family identity is constructed and reconstructed after ABI.

Therefore, this book aims to fill this gap by exploring the identity transition process and bio–psycho–social factors influencing the reconstruction of identity in adults with ABI and their close relatives over time (five years).

References

Beadle, E. J., Ownsworth, T., Fleming, J., & Shum, D. (2016). The impact of traumatic brain injury on self-identity: A systematic review of the evidence for self-concept changes. *Journal of Head Trauma Rehabilitation*, 31(2), E12–E25.

Cantor, J. B., Ashman, T. A., Schwartz, M. E., Gordon, W. A., Hibbard, M. R., Brown, M., et al. (2005). The role of self-discrepancy theory in understanding post-traumatic brain injury affective disorders: A pilot study. *Journal of Head Trauma Rehabilitation*, 20(6), 527–543.

Carpenter, C. (1994). The experience of spinal cord injury: The individual's perspective – implications for rehabilitation practice. *Physical Therapy*, 74 (7), 614–628.

Cloute, K., Mitchell, A., & Yates, P. (2008). Traumatic brain injury and the construction of identity: A discursive approach. *Neuropsychological Rehabilitation*, 18(5/6), 651–670.

Ellis-Hill, C., Payne, S., & Ward, C. (2008). Using stroke to explore the Life Thread Model: An alternative approach to understanding rehabilitation following an acquired brain injury. *Disability & Rehabilitation*, 30(2), 150–159.

Glintborg, C. (2016). Disabled & not normal. Identity construction of adults following an Acquired Brain Injury. *Narrative Inquiry*, 25(1), 1–22.

Gracey, F., Palmer, S., Rous, B., Psailia, K., Shaw, K., O'Dell, J., et al. (2008). Feeling part of things: Personal construction of self after brain injury. *Neuropsychological Rehabilitation*, 18(5/6), 627–650.

Johnson, M. V., Goverover, Y., & Dijkers, M. (2005). Community activities and individuals' satisfaction with them: Quality of life in the first year after traumatic brain injury. *Physical Medicine and Rehabilitation*, 86(4), 735–745.

Jumisko, E., Lexell, J., & Soderberg, S. (2005). The meaning of living with traumatic brain injury in people with moderate to severe traumatic brain injury. *Journal of Neuroscience Nursing*, 37(1), 42–50.

Levack, W. M., Kayes, N. M., & Faydl, J. K. (2010). Experience of recovery and outcome following traumatic brain injury: A metasynthesis of qualitative research. *Disability and Rehabilitation*, 32(12), 986–999.

Moldover, J. E., Goldberg, K. B., & Prout, M. F. (2004). Depression after traumatic brain injury: A review of evidence for heterogeneity. *Neuropsychology Review*, 14(3), 143–154.

Morris, Y. D., Prior, L., Shoumitro, D., Lewis, G., Mayle, W., Burrow, C. E., & Bryant, E. (2005). Patients' view on outcome following head injury: a qualitative study. *BMC Family Practice*, 6(30). Available at: https://bmcfampract.biomedcentral.com/track/pdf/10.1186/1471-2296-6-30.

Nochi, M. (1997). Dealing with the "Void": Traumatic brain injury as a story. *Disability and Society*, 12(4), 533–555.

Nochi, M. (1998). "Loss of self" in the narrative of people with traumatic brain injuries: A qualitative analysis. *Social Science and Medicine*, 46(7), 869–878.

Ownsworth, T. (2014). *Self-identity after brain injury.* New York: Psychology Press.

Ownsworth, T., Fleming, J., Strong, J., Radel, M., Chan, W., & Clare, L. (2007). Awareness typologies, long-term emotional adjustment and psychosocial outcomes following acquired brain injury. *Neuropsychological Rehabilitation*, 17(2), 129–150.

Shadden, B. B. (2005). Aphasia as identity theft. Theory and practice. *Aphasiology*, 19(3–5), 211–223.

Shadden, B. B. & Kosky, P. R. (2007). Social construction of self for persons with aphasia: When language as a cultural tool is impaired. *Journal of Medical Speech-Language Pathology*, 15(2), 99–105.

Silverman, M. (2011). The dignity of struggle. *Topics in Stroke Rehabilitation*, 18(2), 134–138.

3 Narrative identity, discourse, and positioning

Within social science, narratives cannot be reduced to simple recalls of the past. Narratives are retrospective, interpretive compositions that express former events in the light of actual understanding and the evaluation of their meaning (Polkinghorne, 2005).

According to classical narratology, narratives need to have a beginning, a middle, and an ending (a linear perspective). However, classical narratology researchers, who primarily study literature and this view, were challenged by modernists like Virginia Woolf and James Joyce, who undermined the idea of progressive time lines in narratives. Michael André Bernstein (1994) expressed the strongest rejection of linear perspective by highlighting the multiple time perspectives of foreshadowing, back-shadowing, and side-shadowing in literary practices. This means that narratives allow events to be seen in the shadow of the narrator's present, past, and future, just as Polkinghorne (2005) states when he elaborates on the retrospective nature of narratives (that is, the narration of former events in the light of the narrator's present knowledge and understanding).

In Polkinghorne's book *Narrative Knowing and the Human Sciences* (1988), he made a strong argument for the meaning-making process in human existence and the important role narratives play in this process:

> Narratives are a scheme by means of which human beings give meaning to their experience of temporality and personal actions. They provide a framework for understanding the past events of one's life and for planning future actions. They are the primary scheme by which human existence is rendered meaningful. Thus, the study of human beings by the human sciences needs to focus on the realm of meaning in general, and on narrative meaning in particular.
>
> (Polkinghorne, 1988, p. 11)

Thus, a narrative approach offers a systematic perspective on human experience by acknowledging that multiple realities exist rather than just one. For example, professionals and clients who need support do not necessary share the same reality.

Narrative inquiry can seem very subjective, as a study of the individual, but the narratives created by the individual always draw on cultural discourses. Moreover, narrative inquiry focuses on intersubjective relations and how power plays an important role in relations and identity constructions (Foucault, 1969; 1977; 1978). Foucault has helped us to understand how power relations influence the creation, maintenance, and authority of certain knowledge regimes and discourses. Therefore, it is important to understand that self-narratives are always intertwined in psychosocial processes and discourses. With reference to social constructionism, identity is always co-constructed in relation to concrete social interactions (Gergen, 1985). From this perspective, we would not talk about "the brain" or something internal to the individual but should instead focus on social relations. Narratives are always dialogical, and involve continuous interactions between a narrator and his/her audience. In this understanding, identity construction is dependent on accessible discourses.

Thus, narrative inquiry is an approach to the study of human lives conceived as a way of honoring lived experience as a source of important knowledge and understanding; narrative inquiry is a way of understanding experience. It is a collaboration between the researcher and the researched, over time, in a place or series of places, and in social interaction within milieus. As stated by Clandinin and Connelly:

> An inquirer enters this matrix in the midst and progresses in the same spirit, concluding the inquiry still in the midst of living and telling, reliving and retelling, the stories of the experiences that make up people's lives, both individual and social.
>
> (Clandinin & Connelly, 2000, p. 20)

Beginning with a respect for ordinary lived-experience, the focus of narrative inquiry is not only a valorizing of individuals' experiences but also an exploration of the social, cultural, and institutional narratives within which these experiences were constituted, shaped, expressed, and enacted – but in a way that begins and ends that inquiry in the storied lives of the people involved. Narrative inquirers study an individual's experience in the world and, through the study, seek ways of enriching and transforming that experience for themselves and others. Viewed in this way, we can see that a pragmatic ontology of experience is a well-matched theoretical framework for narrative inquiry. Thus, narrative inquiry is an approach to research that recognizes that there are many different ways of interpreting the world and undertaking research, that no single point of view can ever give the entire picture, and that there may be multiple realities.

Why use narrative inquiry in disability research?

Narratives allows us to create order out of chaos. Humans need narratives to bring order to a world that is constantly changing. Ricoeur (1984) uses the term "emplotment" to describe how narrators try to organize sequences logically into meaningful plots. Thus, people often recount narratives when there is a problem, or when something unexpected or out of the ordinary happens.

Health and illness research are areas where narrative work is increasing. One example is the popular use of "illness narratives," which have become part of the way we can relate to our own and others' illnesses. Such narratives can also include those of the relatives of the ABI survivor and the effect on their, the relatives', lives. In the twenty-first century, different media platforms (e.g. websites, blogs, Twitter, Facebook groups, etc.) have become a powerful means of spreading information, sharing emotions, and creating illness communities (Squire, Esin, & Burman, 2013). The medical sociologist Arthur Frank suggested that our interest in illness narratives is connected to the ill person's *desire* to have their suffering recognized (Frank, 1995). A personal illness narrative captures an individual's suffering in everyday situations, in contrast to a medical narrative. During the 1980s, psychologists and sociologists explored the biographical disruptions and reconstitutions that follow a serious long-term illness (Bury, 2001). All types of illnesses affect a person's experience of self and continuity. Thus, illness is often experienced as an intrusive event upon an ongoing life process. In narrative terms, the basic narrative threads of a person's life become broken and need to be reconstructed in telling new stories and revising previous stories. In such new story lines, it becomes possible to encompass both the illness and the surrounding life events. The anthropologist and "narrativist," Mattingly, also describes how story-making and narratives are influential factors in reconstructing identity after illness Mattingly (2000). According to Mattingly, telling a story about your illness can have a healing effect.

Narratives are one of the most important ways for us to make sense of our experiences. When ill, narratives offer an experiential space where an individual can weave together personal and medical concerns and integrate them in their life story, in order to figure out what their illness means for them and what can be done about it. Without the capacity to narrate, this process becomes difficult. The impact of communication disability on self-identity has received considerable attention in research investigating adjustment to aphasia (Shadden, 2005; Shadden & Koski, 2007; Silverman, 2011). For persons with aphasia, their renegotiation of identity is dependent on how they, and their close relatives, adapt to communication difficulties, and narratives can play an important role in this process (Shadden, 2005).

However, there is an implicit assumption that individuals with neurological disabilities might find it hard to remember or narrate their past and may be unable to define a sense of self or be agentic. By contrast, focusing on the person with the disorder as a participant engaged in interaction helps us conceptualize the consequences of the neurological disorder less as an isolated problem, but rather as something that is dealt with in everyday interactions together with other persons (Hyden, 2014). New trends in narrative inquiry include studies on narrative identity in individuals with neurological diseases (e.g. brain injury or Alzheimer's disease). A lot of research in neurological diseases has focused on describing and explaining declines in cognitive and linguistic abilities. In comparison, only a small amount of research has focused on the ways in which persons with neurological diseases cope with these losses. Therefore, adopting a narrative approach helps us understand the role of social interaction in coping with neurological diseases. In a unique study, Kemper, Lyons, and Anagnopoulos (1995) found that:

> Patients with Alzheimer's disease are able to communicate more effectively with their spouses' help and assistance than they are able to alone. Spouses can provide contextual cues for the participants, settings, and significant events in the lives of the patient with Alzheimer's disease.
>
> (Kemper et al., 1995, p. 219)

These findings are in line with sociocultural traditions. For example, Vygotsky argued that the interaction between persons is the base for the child's (and adult's) cognitive, linguistic, and social development (Bruner, 1985; Lave & Wenger, 1991). Narrative inquiry has also been used to explore children's experiences – for example, their experiences of school (Westling Allodi, 2002), reading (Davis, 2007), bullying (Bosacki, Marini, & Dane, 2006), sexual abuse (Mossige, Jensen, Gulbrandsen, Reichelt, & Tjersland, 2005) – as well as identity construction and meaning-making in children with speech and language disorders (Lyons & Roulstone, 2017). The narrative approach allows for a rich description of experiences and an exploration of the meanings that the participants derive from their experiences. Narrative inquiry amplifies voices that may have otherwise remained silent. It utilizes story-telling as a way of communicating the participants' realities, to allow a greater and more in-depth understanding of the particulars of the participants' points of view. The knowledge gained can offer the reader a deeper understanding of the subject material, and extra insight in how to apply the stories to their own context. Narrative inquiry has an underlying philosophy that enables the illumination of real people in real settings through the "painting" of their stories.

Narratives, particularly self-narratives, are especially suitable for studying topics related to identity. The increasing popularity of the study of self-narratives has led to various different approaches to narrative analysis in the last few decades. Research on identities and acquired brain injury (ABI) reveals a growing interest in the co-construction of identity of adults with ABI.

The application of a narrative approach is becoming a valuable tool for inquiry in this area. The contribution of the narrative approach to identity is that it replaces the question of whether an individual is the same across time, or whether they have changed, with an analysis of how people *navigate* this identity dilemma and what influences this process. The way in which people do so, trying to weave past and present into some more or less coherent whole, is reflected in their narrative (Bamberg, De Fina, & Schriffrin, 2011).

As an approach to narrative identity, this book draws on discursive psychology (Davies & Harré, 1990; Potter & Wetherell, 1987). This means that identity is understood as constructed in discourse, as negotiated between speaking subjects in social contexts, and as emergent. This contrasts with a more traditional view of identity as being self-contained (*having* identity) with the consequence that the means by which an individual generates his/her own individuality and character is seen as a personal identity project; here, the focus is on the process (De Fina, Schiffrin, & Bamberg, 2006; Bamberg, et al., 2011). According to Bamberg (2011), any claim of identity will face three dilemmas: (1) successful diachronic navigation between constancy and change; (2) the establishment of a synchronic connection between sameness and difference (between self and other); and (3) the management of agency between the double arrow of a person-to-world versus world-to-person directional fit (Bamberg, 2011, p. 6).

"Dominant discourses" or "master narratives" are also taken up in a type of discourse analysis called "positioning theory" (Bamberg, 2003; Bamberg & Georgakopoulou, 2008; Davies & Harré, 1990).

Positioning theory refers broadly to the close inspection of how speakers describe people and their actions in one way rather than another and, by doing so, perform discursive actions that result in acts of identity (Davies & Harré, 1990, p. 46).

In summary, the theoretical background aligns with the assumption that there is change going on in everyday encounters, in mundane situations, throughout the whole of a person's life. It differentiates from life-span psychology, in that the changes that are taking place are micro changes, and not big changes, where we (in retrospective reflection) think we have changed from one person to another. But there are micro processes within which change typically takes place. And this is exactly where change and consistency work together. In my research, I have investigated how micro processes constitute change, within the contexts where a person comes into being and where a person becomes a social being. That person is the landscape within which development is happening, and then, in turn, it becomes a place for inquiry. This is where the issue of identity and identity formation are at the core. In identity formation, one has to continually navigate between what remains constant, and what changes.. This is at the core of developmental studies, and also at the core of what Bamberg (2011; 2016) refers to as identity formation processes, where a sense of self emerges in these formative processes. Identity is achieved in situated practices in everyday mundane interactions, through small and fragmented stories, in contrast to the big stories that traditionally proliferate in confessional and institutional situations.

References

Bamberg, M. (2003). Positioning with Davie Hogan: Stories, tellings, and identities. In C. Daiute & C. Lightfoot (Eds.), *Narrative analysis: Studying the development of individuals in society* (pp. 135–157). London: Sage.

Bamberg, M. (2011). Who am I? Narration and its contribution to self and identity. *Theory & Psychology*, 21(1), 3–24.

Bamberg, M., De Fina, A., & Schiffrin, D. (2011). Discourse and identity construction. In. S. J. Schwartz et al. (Eds.). *Handbook of identity theory and research* (pp. 1–23). New York: Springer.

Bamberg, M. & Georgakopoulou, A. (2008). Small stories as a new perspective in narrative and identity analysis. *Text & Talk – An Interdisciplinary Journal of Language, Discourse & Communication Studies*, 28(3), 377–396.

Bernstein, M. A. (1994). *Foregone conclusions: against apocalyptic history.* Berkeley, CA: University of California Press.

Bosacki, S., Marini, Z., & Dane, A. (2006). Voices from the classroom: pictorial and narrative representations of children's bullying experiences. *Journal of Moral Education*, 35(2), 231–245.

18   *Theoretical frameworks and methods*

Bruner, J. (1985). *Child's talk. Learning to use language.* New York: W. W. Norton.

Bury, M. (2001). Illness narratives: fact or fiction?. *Sociology of Health and Illness,* 23(3), 263–285.

Clandinin, D. J. & Connelly, M. (2000). *Narrative inquiry: Experience and story in qualitative research.* San Francisco, CA: Jossey-Bass.

Davies, B. & Harré, R. (1990). Positioning: The discursive production of selves. *Journal for the Theory of Social Behavior,* 20(1), 43–63.

Davis, P. (2007). Storytelling as a democratic approach to data collection: Interviewing children about reading. *Educational Research,* 49(2), 169–184.

De Fina, A., Schiffrin, D., & Bamberg, M. (2006). Introduction. In A. De Fina, D. Schiffrin, & M. Bamberg (Eds.), *Discourse and identity* (pp. 1–23). Cambridge, UK: Cambridge University Press.

Foucault, M. (1969). *The archaeology of knowledge.* New York: Routledge.

Foucault, M. (1977). *Discipline and punish: The birth of the prison.* New York: Random House.

Foucault, M. (1978). *The history of sexuality (Vol. 1).* New York: Pantheon Books.

Frank, A. W. (1995). *The wounded storyteller: Body, illness, and ethics.* Chicago, IL: University of Chicago Press.

Gergen, K. (1985). The social constructionist movement in modern psychology. *American Psychologist,* 40(3), 266–274.

Hyden, L. C. (2014). How to do things with others: Joint activities involving persons with Alzheimer's disease. In L. C. Hyden, H. Lindeman, & J. Brockmeir (Eds.) *Beyond loss: dementia, identity, personhood* (pp. 137–154). New York: Oxford University Press

Kemper, S., Lyons, K., & Anagnopoulos, C. (1995). Joint story-telling by Alzheimer's patients and their spouses. *Discourse Processes,* 20(2), 205–217.

Lave, J. & Wenger, E. (1991). *Situated Learning. Legitimate Peripheral Participation.* New York: Cambridge University Press.

Lyons, R., & Roulstone, S. (2017). Labels, identity and narratives in children with primary speech and language impairments. *International Journal of Speech-Language Pathology,* 19(5), 503–518.

Mattingly, C. (2000). Emergent narratives. In Mattingly, C. & L. Garro (Eds.): *Narrative and the Cultural Construction of Illness and Healing* (pp. 181–211). Berkeley, CA: University of California Press.

Mossige, S., Jensen, T., Gulbrandsen, W., Reichelt, S., & Tjersland, O. A. (2005). Children's narratives of sexual abuse – what characterises them and how do they contribute to meaning-making? *Narrative Inquiry,* 15(2), 377–404.

Polkinghorne, D. E. (1988). *Narrative Knowing and the Human Sciences.* Albany, NY: State University of New York Press.

Polkinghorne, D. E. (2005). Language and meaning: Data collection in qualitative research. *Journal of Counselling Psychology,* 52(2), 137–145.

Potter, J. & Wetherell, M. (1987). *Discourse and social psychology. Beyond attitudes and behaviour.* London: Sage.

Ricoeur, P. (1984). *Time and narrative.* Chicago, IL: University of Chicago Press.

Shadden, B. B. (2005). Aphasia as identity theft. Theory and practice. *Aphasiology*, 19(3–5), 211–223.

Shadden, B. B. & Koski, P. R. (2007). Social construction of self for persons with aphasia: When language as a cultural tool is impaired. *Journal of Medical Speech-Language Pathology*, 15(2), 99–105.

Silverman, M. (2011). The dignity of struggle. *Topics in Stroke Rehabilitation*, 18(2), 134–138.

Squire, C., Esin, C., & Burman, C. (2013). "You are here." Visual autobiographies, cultural-spatial positioning, and resources for urban living. *Sociological Research Online*, 18(3), 1. Available at: http://www.socresonline.org.uk/18/3/1.html.

Westling Allodi, M. (2002). Children's experiences of school: narratives of Swedish children with and without learning difficulties. *Scandinavian Journal of Educational Research*, 46(2), 181–205.

4 Establishing first contact, facing professional barriers, and handling "wild" data

With rehabilitation moving from a clinical to a more holistic point of view, and thereby moving into the outpatient domain, it calls for new research designs that are sensitive to the living environment of people with disabilities and the use of a more holistic approach. Moreover, there is also the need to meet the increased importance of active consumer participation in disability research, which is still lacking. When moving into the outpatient domain and into the living environment of adults with acquired brain injury, new challenges emerge for researchers, and the client–professional position can disappear in natural (non-clinical) surroundings.

This chapter describes the ethical concerns and barriers I met while carrying out data collection in the private homes of adults with acquired brain injury (ABI) and their close relatives.

Establishing first contact

When I was preparing for data collection, I found there to be a lack of information on how first contact is established with patients in an outpatient domain and also, on the whole, in both qualitative and quantitative research literature. I had a list of patients hospitalized in a certain hospital who had suffered from a moderate or severe ABI. The initial interview was done when the person was still hospitalized, however, the second and third interviews were done in their private homes. This meant, I had to contact each individual and ask them to participate again in the research project one and five years after the initial interview. Usually, ABI studies only recruit informants who are in some sort of institutional or clinical setting (e.g. hospital or rehabilitation center) and are therefore easier to approach, since they are either seen every day or have frequent appointments to attend. I felt that I faced a certain barrier when contacting the patients in their home surroundings, and I will explore this challenge throughout the chapter. I thought of various ways of re-establishing contact, such as: the discharging hospital could send their former patients an invitation letter; I could send them a letter myself; I could telephone them, etc. In ABI research, and disability research in general, there are several ethical concerns to keep in mind: these adults had suffered from ABI; they could still be in a fragile position; and they may be dealing with cognitive, physical, or psychological consequences. With these considerations in mind, my conclusion was not to burden these adults more than absolutely necessary. I feared that by sending them a letter, the answer rate would be very low because of the possible cognitive deficits in memory or executive function. Furthermore, if the hospital were to telephone on my behalf and specific questions regarding the research project were raised, the hospital might not be able to answer those questions. I therefore decided that I would contact the informants myself, by telephone.

Facing professional barriers – doing "muddy" interviews and handling "wild" data

> I think the most general view is that the only instrument that is sufficiently complex to comprehend and learn about human existence is another human. And so what you use is your own life and your own experiences in the world.
>
> (Lave & Kvale, 1995, p. 220)

In Lippke & Tanggaard (2013), the term "muddy" is used in relation to interviews. The concept of a "muddy interview" is introduced to draw attention to:

> situations in which interviewer and interviewee, intentionally or not, break the norms of interviewing, muddy the conversation and change it into something apparently quite different.
>
> (Lipke & Tanggaard, 2013, p. 137)

The clinical distance you have when you meet informants on neutral ground in a working office, a clinic, or in other settings of the public health and social system, disappear when you enter the private sphere. You see the informant in their entirety and in their personal context and surroundings.

I was invited into the informant's home, offered coffee and cake, and saw the family photographs on the wall, which already included narratives. Moreover, I heard snippets of people's life stories. Some had (or used to have) their businesses at home, which also contained a story. Data is to be found everywhere when you are invited into the private sphere; you observe things, possibly the things that the informants are no longer able to do (e.g.. cleaning or doing the laundry). How do you handle this with respect? I faced these sorts of situations throughout my data collection. In one home, for example, an informant excused the mess in their house by blaming their dog. As a dog owner myself, I know that a dog would not have made such a mess and certainly could not be blamed for the dirty laundry. It can be very difficult to cross personal boundaries with informants, particularly when broaching sensitive topics such as emotions and emotional distress. As a researcher it feels like you are crossing personal and professional boundaries in asking these sorts of questions, because the generic interview scenario and relationship is broken. You become humble and lose your professional shield and the power that lies therein. From being a researcher who takes the lead and controls the process, you instead take the more challenging role of being a guest. This new position changes the relationship and inevitably helps it to become more equal – some of the informants had almost forgotten that I was there as a researcher. One expressed it like this: "*You just sit here and hope that somebody comes by. It has been nice talking to you ... please come again for coffee.*" Being able to do this five-year follow-up study, gave me a unique opportunity to follow the life-path of adults after ABI and to become close with them.

Follow-up studies focusing on quality of life and emotional consequences are sparse within neurorehabilitation. Within a five-year time frame, depression, divorce, loss of jobs, friends, and social status are often factors creating further unwanted change and distress after ABI. As a researcher you meet individuals who are at different stages of coping with these changes. As a researcher within psychology, you must navigate a challenging identity dilemma yourself. That is, navigating the dilemma of being a researcher, therapist, or a friend.

Time

Time was yet another factor that became "muddy" when moving into the outpatient domain. The interview was set to take between 45 and 60 minutes, but when you choose to make the data collection in the informant's own home, timings can easily become compromised if the conversation goes off-topic – and it is important to respect that you are a guest in someone else's home. Therefore, the majority of these interviews lasted about two hours each. If I had been interviewing in a clinical setting, each interview would probably have lasted 30–45 minutes. In addition, several of the informants expressed that it was nice to have someone asking them "how they were feeling." A lot of people asked them "how they were doing," but not about their feelings. Thus, it was important to recognize that the interview itself might become an intervention and I needed to create time for emphatic wrap-ups.

References

Lave, J. & Kvale, S. (1995). What is anthropological research? An interview with Jean Lave by Steinar Kvale. *Qualitative Studies in Education*, 8(3), 219–228.
Lippke, L. & Tanggaard, L. (2013). Leaning in to "muddy" interviews. *Qualitative Inquiry*, 20(2), 136–143.

Part II

The challenges in navigating identity in individuals with ABI and their close relatives

The following chapters unfold emergent themes found among the 82 individuals with ABI and 40 relatives studied. The themes are related to identity (re)construction at different time periods from the subacute hospitalization phase up to five years post-injury. An additional study on the role of peer support in identity reconstruction is also included, to explore this topic further.

5   Identity constructions through a pair of warped glasses

This chapter looks into how identity is constructed and (co)constructed in a five-year time span. Accounts from persons with acquired brain injury (ABI) will give a nuanced view of each individual's ongoing and changing responses to diagnostic labels over time and how a diagnosis (and their experience of illness) can touch on a person's sense of identity and loss of self, and their process of narrative reconstruction.

Based on subjective experiences from almost all informants, I developed the "ABI lens" (Glintborg, Fønsbo, & Fønsbo 2018). This model (Figure 5.1) illustrates that, once diagnosed with a brain injury, this label can actually become the overriding means of defining a person's identity. Professionals' reification of the diagnosis of brain injury can be oppressive because it subjugates humanity, with the result that everything a person does can be interpreted as part of the neurological disability. It starts with professionals, and later friends, family, colleagues, and others, who put on a pair of warped glasses and begin to view behavior through the lens of disability. As illustrated in the model, a person can be forgetful, extroverted, outspoken, or impulsive pre-injury. However, once diagnosed with ABI, these same qualities can be interpreted through the lens of brain injury and reported as ABI symptoms. This way of categorizing the behavior of ABI survivors is oppressive, restrictive, and ultimately dehumanizing, as their individuality is reduced to a generic diagnosis. If a person challenges this and says "*No, this distorted image is not me*" or "*I had these qualities pre-injury, thus they are not symptoms of ABI,*" then these sorts of responses may well be interpreted as further evidence of their disability. In other words, professionals suggest that the person lacks insight into the fact that he or she is ill.

The point is not to undermine the cognitive consequences of ABI, but to point out the potential risk of seeing *all* behavior as pathological symptoms. For instance, the majority of ABI survivors in my study felt that they had become more sensitive or emotional. However, the response

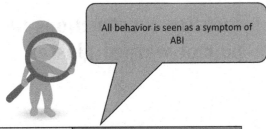

All behavior is seen as a symptom of ABI

Pre ABI	Post ABI
Forgetful = a personal quality	Forgetful = symptom of ABI
Lacking overview = a personal quality	Lacking overview = symptom of ABI
Extrovert/outspoken = a personal quality	Extrovert/outspoken = symptom of ABI
Changed self after a traumatic event (e.g. death of loved one) – a natural process after psychological trauma	Changed self after a neurological and psychological traumatic event (ABI) – a neurological symptom
Impulsive = a personal quality	Impulsive = a symptom of ABI

(Glintborg, 2018)

Figure 5.1 The ABI lens
Source: Glintborg, 2018.

they often got from professionals was that it was quite normal to suffer from emotional lability due to their neurological condition. These narratives exemplify how a medical gaze comes to prevail, and how a dominating diagnostic language is used when one is attempting to make sense of emotional distress. These narratives also demonstrate how difficult it is to stick to an interpretation of one's agony when it deviates from the dominant diagnostic categories within the ABI community.

This feeling of being viewed through the ABI lens took place in various settings, as we shall see:

> *I'm categorized as "brain damaged" and it affects the way people talk to you. For instance, they* [the professionals] *say "are you sure of this" … "we do not think so."*
> (Kevin, 2015, research interview)

Often, Kevin felt that he had to persuade professionals that what he was saying was true. He continued with another example:

> *At some point, I was convinced that the professionals had not informed me of something regarding my training but their answer was that "well, you have a bad memory" so every time I'm seen as*

brain injured. I'm no longer taken seriously. My wife does not think my memory is that bad … it is disrespectful.

(Kevin, 2015, research interview)

The anthropologist Emily Martin argues that a new subject position is brought about when a physician diagnoses a person. You are no longer a person with difficult life problems and problematic feelings, but you have become someone who is living under the description of a particular diagnosis (Martin, 2007). That means that the individual may adopt the diagnostic language and the treatment offered by medicine in their aspiration to make sense of their suffering. The extent to which an individual identifies with their diagnosis varies from case to case, as does the importance of the diagnosis for the person's self-image. Some of the participants in my study fiercely opposed ABI diagnosis, since it was experienced as pathologizing how they felt. Many could not recognize themselves with ABI and therefore put up a fight against the biomedical explanatory framework that was presented to them by medical authorities. However, some gradually experienced an increasing ambiguity, and the diagnosis gradually started to enter their self-understanding and worked as a significant component in combination with other categories outside the diagnostic domain. In the following example, we see how the limitations of ABI, as defined by professionals with diagnostic language, are internalized in Eric's own self narratives:

E: … and in X [name of the rehabilitation center] I had several discussions with the physiotherapists. I told them, "It does not look nice when I walk. It looks disabled." And then they would say to me, "Well you *are* disabled. So it's very natural."

I: And what do you think?

E: And I am. So I can … I must agree with them … that I am ….

(Eric, 2013, research interview)

Here we get a chance to see how the identity, *disabled*, is co-constructed. At first, Eric constructs and positions the way he walks as disabled by saying "*it looks disabled.*" However, the physiotherapist at the center does not accept this positioning of his walk as disabled and, therefore, offers a new position to Eric, switching the pronoun from *it* to *you* and saying "*you are disabled.*" I, however, position Eric as someone who has agency to still decide which position he takes on when I ask him "*what do you think*"; he does not automatically need to accept this offered position as disabled, and still has a choice to position himself in a different way.

Despite this offer, Eric takes on the position offered by the physiotherapist in saying "*I must agree with them … that I am ….*"

It is noteworthy that Eric suggests that the way he walks is "not normal" in a context based on the physical aspects of his impairment. According to post-structuralism and a social constructionist approach, you can see Eric's conclusions as negotiated and constructed in relation to the environment. In Eric's own description of the problem, he positions himself as distanced from the physical problem in saying: "*It* [the walk] *looks disabled.*" However, when a physiotherapist constructs Eric as someone who *is* disabled, Eric accepts this position. The physiotherapist draws on a medical understanding of disability. In this understanding a disability is closely related to the pathology of the body. Eric's sense of self is, thereby, in this discourse, closely related to *his* body.

However, these negotiations do not only take place in interactions with professionals. They also take place in a complex network in which medical authorities, workplaces, relatives, and diagnostic cultures all play a crucial part when ABI diagnosis is negotiated.

Nick talked about how he experienced returning to work:

> *I could see they* [colleagues] *were thinking "you've had a stroke, you are brain injured now" and they kept their distance from me.*
>
> (Nick, 2015, research interview)

Also, relatives can adopt the ABI lens:

> *I haven't paid so much attention to his behavior before the injury – there is a risk that I see things that might always have been a quality of his. Maybe he has always been forgetful and lacked oversight, but I haven't looked at it in this way.*
>
> (Karen, 2016, research interview)

Here we see how Karen adopts the lens and now looks at behavior as possible symptoms. Many partners described this new superpower as the ability to see symptoms and observe everything in various situations and intervene if they felt that the partner fell out of the "ordinary" norm for good behavior in a certain situation, or if anybody mistreated him or her. They not only observe the behavior of their partner, but also how the surrounding people react to their partner. Is anything different than before? Is the partner behaving the same way? Are friends behaving the same way or differently now? Are they communicating with the partner in a different way? Are they treating them differently?

The following two examples illustrate how a relative intervenes in two different situations. In the first extract, we see how Hanne, who is married to Eric, observes and intervenes during the third interview I had with the couple:

> I'm interviewing Eric and his wife Hanne and we're having coffee. Eric is very enthusiastic and talks a lot. Suddenly his wife Hanne interferes and address Eric "*You need to eat your cake. You talk so much that your cakes are piling up*" [on his plate]. The situation becomes a little awkward and Eric stops talking and start eating his cakes.
>
> (Field observation, 2017)

Before Eric suffered from ABI, Hanne would presumably not interfere during a coffee setting, but the risk of Eric stepping out of the norm or discourse of "how to do a coffee situation" because he now has ABI might make her intervene. However, what actually happens in this situation is that it creates an even more awkward situation and attention is drawn to Eric, which is what Hanne presumably intended to avoid.

In the second excerpt, we see how Hanne intervenes toward the researcher in the first interview:

> I get the impression that Hanne is very attentive toward Eric. She looks at him and tries to read him. She seems very protective toward him in her behavior. Therefore, when I want to pour Eric a cup of tea, it surprises me that she immediately intervenes by saying: "*You should ask him first.*"
>
> (Field observation, 2015)

In this text, the researcher positions Hanne as someone being very aware of how to treat Eric with respect and not as disabled, e.g. you do not just pour tea without asking. Even though the approach between Eric and Hanne seems equal, Hanne has a meta-perspective on what is going on, both in relation to herself and Eric, and also toward others: for example, in how she supervises the researcher in this situation. This superpower could affect their identity as a couple. Additionally, this superpower introduces the risk of creating an imbalance in their relationship. The person with ABI is being supervised and the relative intervenes toward the person or the environment. But how does it feel to be supervised as a person with ABI, who might already feel vulnerable and struggle with shame or guilt? What kind of new identity is taken on by relatives and with what consequences?

Identity (re)constructions in power-imbalanced relations

Power imbalance in professional–ABI survivor and relative–ABI survivor relationships can affect identity reconstruction both in persons with ABI and their close relatives. There might be a clash of perceptions in various settings and situations between professionals and/or relatives and persons with ABI during their most vulnerable times. The same situation can be experienced very differently depending on whose eyes we see the situation through. For instance, in the preface, we see two different perspectives on the same situation in that Lillian:

> ... *describes herself as being super happy to be alive and she is happy to see Lars (her husband) again. It is like we are falling in love all over again, she says. However, Lillian is told by a neuropsychologist that she seems almost artificially happy, and it is noted in her journal that they* [the professionals] *must be aware of behavioral changes.*
>
> (Lillian, 2012, research interview)

Can either of these two perspectives be more accurate than the other? Because of the enormous power in professional–survivor relationships, there is a risk that the professional's interpretations and narratives about a person with ABI can become the truth and the narratives of persons with ABI can be silenced. What happens here is a "double silencing." The first silencing is imposed by the professional, during neurorehabilitation, who stops the person being heard. The second silencing is imposed when this person's experience of neurorehabilitation is ignored, or not enquired into, and the professional's interpretation of the outcome of neurorehabilitation is prescribed as the only truth.

There are various examples of professionals' interpretations becoming the official story while the stories, the voices, and the experiences of disabled people and relatives are silenced. This raises worrying questions such as: Who gets to say if the neurorehabilitation is working? Whose directives are followed and whose are silenced? Who gets to say if professional help is helpful?

Silencing people with disabilities through the assertion of the expert's professional opinion occurs regularly, especially in cases of neurological or psychiatric disabilities where insight issues appear, and the survivor's personal judgment is considered to be unreliable. It is not uncommon for an expert to declare that a person is making good progress while they are working in a sheltered workshop, but, in reality, the person with the disability feels like a failure or is ashamed because they are not working in a "real" job. This shame can also be experienced by relatives, e.g. *"Before my husband was an engineer, now he has casual employment,"* or *"Before he was the party starter, but now he might fall out of conversations or say inadequate things."* This has an impact on a couple's identity.

Communication: childish talk

The form of communication can also indicate an imbalance in relationships. A majority of participants in my research expressed how they were approached and addressed like children (as if to indicate that they were not intellectually competent). One of the participants expressed it like this:

> *I was yelled at like a child at the rehabilitation center when I did not follow my* [training] *schedule.* [He continued] *I don't think they respected my opinions because of my brain injury.*
> (James, 2015, research interview)

Stanley also addressed the communication form:

> *My God, I'm so tired of their childish talk and infantile metaphors. I'm not stupid. I'm a normal human being and an adult who had an injury. That doesn't make me an imbecile, so please stop treating me like one. Just talk to me as you would talk to someone who had a broken ankle in an orthopedic ward. Like a human. They think that there is nothing behind … maybe a child, but they are wrong. Inside there is a regular grownup with thoughts and a mind.*
> (Stanley, 2018, research interview)

> *All the professionals at the ward have entered my room the last couple of days, they all greet me nicely, but use "Stanley" at both ends of all their sentences and they address me like I am a four-year-old. It is horrible. This is not a kindergarten. And I don't want to meet any more strangers. "Hi Stanley! So nice you made it here, Stanley." Thank you, Thank you. They talk to me as if they have known me for years. They lean their heads and talk abnormally loudly, abnormally slowly, and incredibly articulated, as if I don't understand what they are saying. But I do. I understand everything. But yet they talk like this. Just weird. Just weird. I want to scream*

to them: "speak normally to me, woman!" I have not lost my mind. And no I have not become aggressive either, I'm just tired and not used to being spoken to like this.

(Stanley, 2018, research interview)

When professionals position themselves in an overfamiliar way or as if friends, there is a risk that the communication form can be experienced as indulgent. In both cases, ABI survivors have felt that they have been spoken to like a child or an idiot. Among professionals there can be remarks exchanged like "think of him like a three-year-old." The problem here is that it disempowers the adult individual.

References

Glintborg, C., Fønsbo, E., & Fønsbo, S. (2018). *Hovedbrud. Hjerneskade fra tre perspektiver.* Frederiksberg, Denmark: Frydenlund.

Martin, E. (2007). Violence, language, and everyday life. *American Ethnologist*, 34(4), 741–745.

6 Normalization versus pathologizing

With reference to the ABI lens, there is a risk of over-pathologizing normal behavior. Moreover, a risk that neurological knowledge increasingly overshadows other possible ways of understanding mental distress, such as existentially. For persons with acquired brain injury (ABI), it can be a great relief to hear that feelings and behaviors are not so abnormal after all, and that actually they are quite common, as many other people also struggle with the exact same things. This process is called "normalization" and can be used therapeutically to help deconstruct a pathologized identity, as illustrated here in a quotation taken from the interview with Mette:

I: How much has this process affected you psychologically? How are you feeling?

M: It has affected me very much, totally. I have been down 100 times. Then up and down again. I have wanted a divorce, to commit suicide, I just wanted ... to disappear and not come back again. I went to the brain injury rehabilitation center for two years and I saw a psychologist there, and she helped me put a lot of things into place and I don't think I would have been here today, if it wasn't for her ... if she hadn't told me the things she did ... It was groundbreaking ... now I'm starting to get emotional ... She just put so many things into place. Incredible ....

I: What kind of things were groundbreaking?

M: You mean what the psychologist did? Well it had a lot to do with the birth of Mads, because it was such a traumatic event, and I was just ... It was so awful, so horrible, and then she told me things, and told me it was totally okay and it was normal to feel like that and just that ... What a relationship we had. I could talk to her about everything, all kinds of weird things that I felt, and then she just said "it is okay Mette, I have had similar feelings." I will put it like this: if she had not been there, I don't think I would have made it to the other side mentally.

(Mette, 2018, research interview)

In this excerpt we see two core elements: *normalization* and *common humanity* being constructed in a therapeutic setting. When we talk about normalization as a therapeutic tool we do not mean the legitimization of destructive ways of being in the world. We mean building a foundation for positive change by helping a person see, where it is applicable, that those uncomfortable thoughts and motivations do not make them abnormal, but simply human beings struggling to face and overcome existential challenges.

Normalization and validation

Normalization is not to be confused with validation. Validation is about connecting with the unique experience of an individual, whereas normalization is about communicating that other people have the same experience. Normalization can be needed, as seen in the case with Mette, and can also be enormously beneficial. The knowledge that others share the same experiences, can make it seem less extreme or pathological, and can help individuals feel less alone. Anyone who has ever felt behind on a school or work task, and then later discovers that others felt like this too, can understand and appreciate the value of normalization. Similarly, going to a peer group and meeting people with similar issues normalizes and often brings relief (see also Chapter 11). However, there can also be drawbacks to normalization, particularly when it causes invalidation for a person who does not feel that his or her individual experience is adequately acknowledged and shared by others.

Sometimes normalization is not enough. So, what does it mean if other people share this feeling, and what does that have to do with me?

An example of validation, as in the case of Mette, could be to validate that, yes other people share similar experiences, but the exchange between the person with ABI and the professional should also focus on how the experience affects that particular person, not others. For example, "*I can see how debilitating this depression has become, and if that wasn't enough, now you're also struggling with guilt.*" The decision to normalize versus validate is based on and determined by the person's needs. The two techniques can be used successfully in tandem. The important thing is to know the difference between the two. Validation is essential for adults with ABI to be understood. As these adults often come from invalidating environments, validation offers them new ways of understanding (Linehan & Dimeff, 2001).

One of the most important elements of Compassion Focused Therapy (CFT) (Gilbert, 1989) is the recognition of our shared humanity. The psychologist in the quotation includes herself in the suffering, by revealing that she had also experienced the same feelings. Compassion is, by definition, relational. Compassion literally means "to suffer with," which implies a basic mutuality in the experience of suffering. The emotion of compassion springs from the recognition that human experience is imperfect and that we are all fallible. With reference to Bamberg's identity dilemmas, the therapist here constructs a *sameness* with Mette. Here, Mette is not different from others (us vs. them). This approach contrasts with a more traditional and distanced professional/ expert vs. client approach. Mette is not the only one remembering a certain professional from her rehabilitation. Many of the participants in my research also remembered a professional who had a lasting, positive impact on them. These qualities, or ways of interacting with others, form the basis of what Carl Rogers (1980) termed a "way of being," which I will return to in Chapter 12.

References

Bamberg, M. (2011). Who am I? Narration and its contribution to self and identity. *Theory & Psychology, 21*(1), 3–24.

Gilbert, P. (1989). *Human nature and suffering.* London: Routledge.

Linehan, M. M. & Dimeff, L. (2001). Dialectical *Behavior Therapy* in a nutshell. *The California Psychologist, 34*(3), 10–13.

Rogers, C. R. (1980). *A way of being.* Boston, MA: Houghton Mifflin.

7   Same but different

When continuity is threatened

This chapter centers on human development in circumstances where continuity and coherence are at threat and identity needs to be reworked. One of the most striking things in the interviews was the continuous discontinuity described by acquired brain injury (ABI) survivors and the apparent lack of connection between different life domains (pre-injury and post-injury). With reference to Bronfenbrenner's ecological model, the connection between different life domains is central. His second system, "the mesosystem," deals with precisely these relationships between the systems that the individual belongs to, how they mutually influence each other, and the importance of interaction between the systems (Bronfenbrenner, 1979). The importance of coherence between different life domains is not only central within developmental psychology, but it is also considered particularly important when it comes to the treatment of complex and prolonged diseases, as it fundamentally supports the rehabilitation process.

When a person acquires a brain injury, an array of providers will offer their services. These different services come from a variety of organizations, as well as from different sectors. This does, however, raise concerns about the fragmented way in which these services are provided, because this could challenge the continuity of the rehabilitation process. Haggerty et al. (2003) conducted a multidisciplinary review on the concept of "continuity of care," and found two core elements in continuity: (1) care of the individual; and (2) care over time. In care of the individual, the unit of measurement of continuity is the individual experience. Care over time is not seen as a dimension of continuity but as an intrinsic part of it. Traditional measurement focuses on patterns of rehabilitation/care or the outcomes of it but does not measure the experience of rehabilitation or continuity. Instead of adopting traditional approaches, we should therefore focus on how the individual and their relatives experience the integration and coordination of services. In the review the authors concluded:

> Unless we understand the mechanism through which care delivered over time improves outcomes, continuity interventions may be misdirected or inappropriately evaluated.
>
> (Haggerty et al., 2003, p. 1220)

Haggerty et al. (2003) identified three types of continuity: (1) *Informational continuity*, which can be focused on the disease or the person. However, most documentation tends to focus on the medical condition, while information on the person's preferences, values, and life is often accumulated in the primary providers' memory and not written down. (2) *Management continuity* is the requirement that services are delivered in a complementary and timely manner. For instance, shared rehabilitation plans can facilitate management continuity. Moreover, flexibility in adapting rehabilitation to changes in the individual's need is a crucial aspect of management continuity. (3) *Relational continuity* bridges past, present, and future rehabilitation. A consistent core of staff providers is not always achievable, but it is nevertheless of crucial importance to secure a sense of predictability and coherence. The adoption of processes designed to improve continuity, such as coordination, does not in itself equate to continuity. For continuity to exist it has to be linked to the individual's experience of rehabilitation as connected and coherent. For individuals with ABI and their close relatives, the experience of continuity is the perception that providers know their personal preferences, that different providers agree on a rehabilitation plan, and that a provider who knows them will care for them in the future. For providers, the experience of continuity relates to their perception that they have sufficient knowledge and information about a client to best apply their professional competence, and the confidence that their care inputs will be recognized and pursued by others. However, we must be aware that the experience of continuity may differ for the person with a disability and the providers, which poses a challenge to evaluators.

Recent research, based on neuropsychological theories about how the brain is shaped by use, highlights the same issues, namely that stable relationships are essential for the development of healthy neurological functioning (Bath, 2015; Ludy-Dobson & Perry, 2010; Siegel, 2012). ABI survivors may feel better after staying in a neurological ward for a few weeks, as the security and stable relationships there help to provide a sense of well-being. However, since they are quickly discharged into solitude again, according to this framework, it is also natural that the development does not continue, and that momentary improvement does not lead to stable and lasting changes. To achieve lasting changes, there is a need for long-term relationships. Bronfenbrenner's (2005) theory of proximal processes claims that for development to take place, the person must participate in an activity that takes place regularly over a period of time and that involves more people. According to Bronfenbrenner, however, it is not just the duration that is important, but also that the relationship is mutual and characterized by cooperation. Ljungberg, Denhov, and Topor (2015) conducted a meta-analysis of 21 studies to explore what patients experienced as helpful and useful in relation to health professionals. Their findings show that what patients found most useful was spending a lot of time with health professionals, receiving access to resources and support, and having a relationship characterized by mutual cooperation. It is therefore possible that the difference between reciprocity and control in relationships may have contributed to differences in development for ABI survivors.

In response to these challenges, there is a growing international recognition within health care for the need to support service transitions. For example, the Danish Board of Health has published two best practice guidelines for brain injury rehabilitation (Danish Board of Health, 2011a; 2011b). Their common recommendation is coordinated rehabilitation programs to ensure seamless service transitions and continuity of care. A similar undertaking in Norway established coordination reforms. By 2001 it had already been determined that:

> citizens who need long-term coordinated services under the health and care services law, the specialist health services law and the mental health services law have the right to have an individual care plan.
> (Norwegian Ministry of Health and Care Services, 2010–2011)

Enactment of an individual care plan has several purposes including: ensuring that patients receive comprehensive, coordinated, and individually adjusted services; ensuring real service user involvement; and ensuring collaboration between the patient (and possibly their relatives) and service providers, as well as between service providers.

Coherence can be seen, from a narrative perspective, as the ability to create a coherent narrative. Within this research, we have seen that the person with ABI and their close relatives are not liberated from categorical terms (e.g., normal, disabled, brain damaged, etc.), but by using a narrative approach the individual can still transform the way their sense of self is co-constructed.

To exemplify, the following case study illustrates how an individual navigates dilemmas of coherence, change, and sameness vs. difference over a span of five years. In Chapter 6 we introduced Mette, a young woman in her mid-twenties who lives with her husband Christian and their son Johannes. During her pregnancy, Mette had a stroke (a cerebral thrombosis). I have had three meetings with Mette: the first meeting was two weeks post-injury when she was still hospitalized, the second meeting was one year post-injury, and the third meeting was five years post-injury.

First meeting: two weeks post-injury

I met Mette for the first time during spring 2013. Mette had had a stroke two weeks earlier and was now being observed at a rehabilitation center, following the acute hospitalization phase. Mette was pregnant and was two weeks away from giving birth to her first child.

During the first meeting, Mette expressed that she was happy and relieved that she got off so lightly (with ABI). She frequently found it hard to look at the other patients at the rehabilitation center who were more severely affected by ABI. She seemed happy and cheerful and smiled during the interview. Mette was being discharged later that day after only two weeks at the rehabilitation center, because she had experienced no physical aftereffects from ABI. She agreed with the professional evaluation because she too did not feel that she had had any severe consequences as a result of ABI. During my testing of her (for depression and quality of life) she mentioned that a rehabilitation plan had been made, but Mette said: "*I need very little help*" (Field notes).

The depression test showed no sign of depression and the quality of life (QOL) test showed a high QOL. It was arranged that a nurse from the psychiatric ward (pediatric) would get in touch with Mette when she was to give birth to her son. The doctor had organized this to prevent any delayed psychological reactions during or following labor. However, so far, Mette had not experienced any psychological effects. During the testing, Mette seemed relieved about this, and said: "*Well, you won't find much here*" (Field notes). In connection with the rehabilitation, she explained that she had never felt "lost" (in the sense of not getting what she needed) and that she had received all the support she could wish for.

Second meeting: one year post-injury

About one year later, I met Mette for the second time. A lot had happened in Mette's life since that first meeting. Mette had become a mother and moved to a new house with her husband Christian. However, she was still waiting for clarification regarding her return to work.

The interview began with a question about how Mette felt about her ABI now:

I: Can you tell me a bit more about how you feel about the brain injury today?

M: It burns all the way up here (points at her arms), in the skin. It is resilient, it is sore and so are all of my muscles, there are some big muscular lumps .... There is a constant tension in my leg, so it is also very swollen and sometimes I cannot really go anywhere because I simply feel pain in my entire arm and leg.

I: No. Okay. Is there anything else?

M: Not related to the body.

(Mette, 2015, research interview)

In the first excerpt, Mette focused on the physical consequences. Later in the interview, Mette addressed the psychological aspects as well and said: "*I am not that affected physically. It is highly, highly affecting psychologically.*" Becoming a mother and having ABI was especially difficult:

I: So, which things come to mind, when you think about what it was like, becoming a mother?

M: Well, anxiety, bad conscience, bad conscience, and bad conscience.

I: Yes, okay. How did you experience that?

M: (M is crying). Well, I could not be there for my son, I could not get up at night and nurture him, I could not give him milk and ... And he would just lay there, the little guy, and be all perfect, but I just could not. I have not even been able to go swimming with him, so we have been home a lot. I could not think about meeting the maternity group, and it has been difficult for some (of the other mothers from the maternity group) to understand, that I did not go out with them. So, it has been really hard going from being very, very social to living in a box.

(Mette, 2015, research interview)

When Mette was asked what it was like to become a mother, she answered in two specific terms: (1) *anxiety* and (2) *bad conscience*, of which bad conscience was repeated three times. The depression test conducted at the second meeting indicated that Mette showed signs of severe depression. Furthermore, there was a significant decrease in her psychological and physical QOL compared to the pretesting one year earlier.

At the second meeting, we saw a young woman who, in comparison to the first meeting, suffered from ABI in both a physical and a highly psychological way. Mette constructed herself as an *inadequate* mother, both in relation to her son (not being able to nurture him) and as a social mother (not being a part of the maternity group). Thereby, Mette constructed herself as different from others but, at this second point in time, the positions were negative (whereas at the first meeting she felt different because she had got off so lightly compared to others with ABI). Furthermore, she constructed the transition from being social to "living in a box" as hard. This indicated that Mette could not cope with navigating these identity dilemmas.

Mette was also asked about the future:

I: What thoughts do you have about the future?
M: It is definitely about an acceptance of what is going to happen with my life and a follow-up on that. Will I be a part of a vocational rehabilitation? Or what will happen to me? And what will happen to us?

(Mette, 2015, research interview)

Mette questioned *"What is going to happen with my life?"* and, more specifically, *"What will happen to me?"* and *"What will happen to us?"* several times. These rhetorical questions showed that Mette had accepted what had happened and had actually taken on the more passive position of waiting and standing by, as she was not looking for an answer.

Next in the interview, Mette told us about what she was like at the time when she met her husband, Christian. This was at a time in her life when she used to engage extensively in social activities with her friends. Mette constructed herself as free in this period of time: *"I was the free Mette."* Furthermore, she said:

M: You see, I am the social Mette, who has always been "the clown," who got totally wasted at the disco, right … And now, I cannot even consider having one drink. And sometimes my friends say to me, oh, they miss the old Mette.
I: Do you miss her, Mette?
M: Yes, I miss her so much.

(Mette, 2015, research interview)

Here Mette was struggling with the dilemma of constancy and change (Bamberg, 2011). For instance, she said that she *was* the social Mette (trying to hold on to her coherent identity), in the temporal form of presence, but then went on to describe how she could not go out and have drinks with her friends anymore and how they missed the "old Mette." There was a lost self: the social self. We found that the reconstruction process that Mette engaged in was characterized by much *ambivalence*. For instance, she said:

> *You see, it is a new Mette, that has come ... Who is this new Mette, who is about to come, and will my friends accept the new identity, and will they still see me as who I was before.*
>
> (Mette, 2015, research interview)

Ambivalent accounts and different scenarios were presented here. Mette worried about whether or not her friends would still see her as she was *before* ABI. At the same time, she wondered whether her friends would accept the *new* identity. Furthermore, she was actually presenting three different identities: (1) a Mette who had come, (2) a Mette who was about to come, and (3) the Mette she was before ABI. These accounts reflected the fact that Mette was navigating between different identities: who she had been, who she was, and who she would become. In asking *"Will my friends accept the new identity, and will they still see me as who I was before,"* Mette also constructed a potential risk of losing her social and intimate relationships. Earlier Mette had constructed a loss of the "old Mette," in saying that both she and her friends "miss the old Mette." Moreover, she said: "He [her husband] fell in love with a Mette who is not there anymore. And how does that affect his love for me?" This pointed to the direction that Mette wished to take, in ways that would help her maintain her social and intimate relationships. The analysis showed that this was also why Mette could not quite accept this developing identity (the "new Mette") and therefore held on to who she was (the "old Mette"). However, by constructing such a hope of going back, she also constructed the possibility of being the same, and thereby of being part of the same social environment that she used to.

Third meeting: five years post-injury

In 2018, I saw Mette for the third time, now five years post-injury. Also present at this meeting was Mette's mother, Susan. Mette's status with regard to work had now been clarified: she would not be able to return to work and was now on a disability pension. The interview started out with a question on how Mette was feeling now, five years post-injury:

M: It's still a challenge that I have to take naps, because I think I miss out on things, but it is also more of an everyday thing now ... but I always have an eye on the time.

M: I'm able to do much more than last year. I don't know if it is me accepting things more or because I'm getting to know myself more ... and I do have a huge social network – Mom and Dad, they help me very much and Christian has helped me tremendously. He's always ... he can see "Well Mette now it's time for a nap." I don't need to think of anything, he's just there. And you [talking to her mother, who sits beside her] are so good at saying "I'll pick Johannes up today, so you don't have to worry about that so you can sleep."

(Mette, 2018, research interview)

Mette was very dependent on her mother and would speak with her on the phone several times a day. Her mother had adjusted her work hours so she could help Mette. In general, Mette spoke a lot about how the people surrounding her had helped by showing concern. "*They are so understanding*," she said. She talked about a recent trip to a Danish island with her friends. All the time they took into account that Mette had to go home and take a nap as she could not be out for too long or go to restaurants.

When I asked her more directly how she felt about these specific allowances that friends and family had to make, a conflicting narrative emerged:

I: How do you feel about these concerns people have. Are you comfortable with them?

M: Sometimes. But I think ... Well, I can say that it's great that I can go home and take a nap, but it's also hard. Because, I really want to be part of everything. I really do. I feel that I miss out, because I have to take a nap the whole time and I can't join in. It's so annoying, also because you're so young like me, you just want to be part of it all. So sometimes I'm better at accepting it than others. During the trip to X (mentions the place) I felt really bad about it, and I cried a lot. I just had to go home and fucking sleep ... so when I want to do too much, accepting can be hard.

(Mette, 2018, research interview)

Also, Mette's mother had two narratives – one affirmed that things are good, but the other narrative was about fear, guilt, and anxiety.

During the interview, I turned to Susan and asked if she had received any support:

I: Have you received any support?

S: We were at a meeting where we received information on what a brain injury is, and that was okay, but I did not have the time to think if I should have support or not. First, I had to help Mette, and luckily, I had a very good job and was able to take sick leave. But ... I guess I feel the same way as Mette, but I can control it, because ... Today we have social media, so I can always see if Mette is online or not. If I babysit Johannes, and Mette has the day off [from child care] ... I usually take Johannes when I have days off, so Mette can sleep in. But then she has promised me to go on Facebook every so often, so I can see that she is online. So actually, I also have a form of ... what do you call it ...

M: You are scared. You have anxiety.

S: Yes! At my work, I have said that I have a mobile with me, and it is on the highest volume even though the rules are that phones are not allowed. So, I have a kind of ...

I: You are alert.

S: Yes. Also, in the house, if I hear an ambulance I get up. Even if I see an ambulance on the highway, I have to stop and check if Mette has been online. I can also ... I think that I have let myself in here [Mette's house] just to check if she has slept for six hours, while we have had Johannes.

M: My Mom is the one that suffered the most, not Christian, but Mom. And I remember it also because, when I got sick my Mom planned to come by and say hi, but she did not come because she felt nothing was wrong and instead she drove home.

S: Yes, I thought to myself "You should stop yourself and drive home." I feel guilty today, but I cannot change it now.

M: No, and we have talked about this; you can't blame yourself today ...

M: I wish there could have been some support for my Mom.

(Mette & Susan, 2018, research interview)

These interview conversations illustrate that Susan had actually planned to visit Mette on the day that Mette had her stroke, but in the end had decided not to. Therefore, Mette was alone for quite a while when she suffered from the stroke, which had made the situation more serious. Susan was coping with her fear and compensated for her guilt in different ways. She had various methods in place that allowed her to check on Mette throughout the day, regardless of where she, Susan, was. Mette had promised her mother to be on social media at intervals, so that Susan was able to see that Mette was online and therefore okay. Mette seemed to have accepted this controlling position that her mother had taken on, even though it left her in the position of being a passive recipient. Susan's controlling function did interfere with Mette's private life (Susan would let herself in, Mette had to be online every so often, etc.). Presumably, this might also have affected the relationship between Mette and her husband Christian. During the interview, Mette said several times "*I sound like a five-year-old*," when she heard her mother talk about the different ways she was able to check on Mette. So, in a way, hearing Susan's narrative might have caused some reflection in Mette. Mette referred to her relationship with her Mom as being close prior to her injury; however, now the narration about the relationship ran the risk of unbalancing a previously more equal relationship, shifting it to an adult–child relationship characterized by checking behavior.

A worry was also about Susan ever being off-duty. She was constantly on the alert, with her daily life and work changed and planned around Mette's situation. She seemed to have put her own needs aside in order to be there to support Mette and to prevent a new incident from occurring. Presumably it was also quite stressful to live under such a constant fear. The "online" relief when something happened (e.g. when she heard an ambulance but was able to check that Mette was fine) might have only given a brief respite in her stress levels. So, as Mette put it, her mother could end up being the one that suffered the most, since her life had changed dramatically following Mette's ABI, and yet her mother did not get any support. Mette referred to the psychological support she received as an important turning point: "*I will put it like this; if she* [the psychologist] *had not been there, I don't think I would have made it to the other side mentally*," as described in Chapter 6. But who would help Susan with her changed life, her fear, and her guilt, in order to prevent compassion fatigue or other psychological consequences? I return to guilt and shame and ways to deal with this in Chapter 10.

References

Bamberg, M. (2011). Who am I? Narration and its contribution to self and identity. *Theory & Psychology*, 21(1), 3–24.

Bath, H. (2015). The three pillars of TraumaWise Care: healing in the other 23 hours. *Reclaiming Children and Youth*, 23(4), 5–11.

Bronfenbrenner, U. (1979). *The ecology of human development. Experiments by nature and design*. Cambridge, MA: Harvard University Press.

Bronfenbrenner, U. (ed.) (2005). *Making human beings human: Bioecological perspectives on human development*. Thousand Oaks, CA: Sage Publications.

Danish Board of Health (Sundhedsstyrelsen) (2011a). *Hjerneskaderehabilitering – en medicinsk teknologivurdering* [Brain injury rehabilitation – a medical technology assessment]. Available at: http://sundhedsstyrelsen.dk/publ/Publ2011/MTV/Hjerneskaderehabilitering/Hjerneskaderehabilitering.pdf.

Danish Board of Health (Sundhedsstyrelsen) (2011b). *Forløbsprogram for rehabilitering af voksne med erhvervet hjerneskade*. [Disease management programme for brain injury rehabilitation]. Available at: http://sundhedsstyrelsen.dk/publ/Publ2011/BOS/Hjernetraume/ForloebsprogramVoksneHjernetraume.pdf.

Haggerty, J. L., Reid, R. J., Freeman, G. K., Starfield, B. H., Adair, C. E., & McKendry, R. (2003). Continuity of care: A multidisciplinary review. *British Medical Journal*, 327(7425), 1219–1221.

Ljungberg, A., Denhov, A., & Topor, A. (2015). The art of helpful relationships with professionals: A meta-ethnography of the perspective of persons with severe mental illness. *Psychiatric Quarterly*, 86(4), 471–495.

Ludy-Dobson, C. R. & Perry, B. D. (2010). The role of healthy relational interactions in buffering the impact of childhood trauma. In Gil, E. (Ed). *Working with children to heal interpersonal trauma: The power of play* (pp. 26–43). New York: Guilford Press.

Norwegian Ministry of Health and Care Services (2010–2011). The Coordination Reform, Proper treatment – at the right place and right time. Available at: www.regjeringen.no/contentassets/d4f0e16ad32e4bbd8d8ab5c21445a5dc/en-gb/pdfs/stm200820090047000en_pdfs.pdf/.

Siegel, D. J. (2012). *The developing mind*, 2nd Edition. New York: Guilford Publications.

8 Hope and recovery

Why is hope important to recovery? Because hope is the root of life's energy. Hope is the tenacious pursuit of pathways to a better life, despite the odds. Without hope, there is no recovery.

Prognosis of doom – loss of hope

When people acquire brain injuries, something happens not only to those people's brains and bodies, but also to their future. There is a risk that the future is no longer theirs to make, since it has already been prescribed in a neurological textbook. The future of non-diagnosed people is ambiguous and uncertain. However, once diagnosed with acquired brain injury (ABI), there is a high potential risk that the future is predicted according to one's diagnosis. Professionals can tell people with ABI that they suffer from a chronic condition; some are advised to take early retirement or seek a disability pension. In other words, they are condemned to a life of "handicaptivity." A life devoid of meaning and purpose is stressful. A vegetative life is stressful. A life in handicaptivity, lived out within the confines of the social services landscape, where the only people who spend time with you are people who are paid to be with you – that is stressful – and can affect your identity and quality of life even further. Moreover, the burden of having to rely on disability support from the government can also have a hugely damaging impact on people's identities.

If diagnosed with ABI, you need hopeful messages and positive role models. You need to hear that there are pathways into a meaningful future. There is a need to connect with others in the same situation and who have recovered lives of meaning and purpose. You need to find others who have completed education or returned to work despite ABI. Mead, a key representative of symbolic interactionism, highlights that when we talk to others, we ourselves are also recipients of our own message, while also creating our own self through interaction with others – so that the self is a social self (Mead, 1913). Our "self" interacts with other "selves," such as when a person with ABI speaks empathetically to and about other persons with similar needs, and hears others do the same. This provides signals to the person themselves, both in relation to the person they are, and how they expect others to relate to their problems. In my research, it was also clear that, for many participants, interacting with peers was important. I explore this topic further in Chapter 11.

Hope is an important part of the rehabilitation process. Hope and motivation are uniquely bound together. However, several informants revealed that hope was continually being destroyed throughout their recovery by professionals:

> *They* [the professionals] *destroy people's hope and the motivation you have to get better. I was informed that I should not expect more progress* [five years after ABI]. *It's important to have hope. The improvement you make is important. I can still see improvement from week to week.*
>
> (Eric, 2017, research interview)

Here we see how Eric experiences hope being destroyed or undermined by professionals, thereby also destroying his motivation. Eric experiences improvement from week to week, but this personal experience is overruled (silenced) by the professionals' assertions that he should not expect any more progress.

Maintaining hope and seeing possibilities for further development play an important role in coping with and recovering from ABI. Therefore, it can seem contradictory that the assessment of individuals with ABI during the rehabilitation process focuses on abilities that they have lost, rather than what they are still able to do, as expressed by Jasper in the following quote:

> *They* [professionals] *have been busier showing me what I'm not able to do.*
>
> (Jasper, 2017, research interview)

Within neuropsychology, it has been seen as good practice to confront ABI survivors with their disabilities, as it is thought that this can lead to a greater insight and acceptance of their difficulties and thus to a greater motivation to explore their limitations. In practice, however, it appears that confrontations do not necessarily lead to increased motivation. On the contrary, they can lead either to individuals losing motivation and giving up, or to mental resistance (Rollnick, Miller, & Butler, 2013). Therefore, we might need to rethink the concept of insight.

With reference to Sedikides and Gregg (2008), a rejection of this kind of insight and the maintenance of narratives that hold on to prior competencies can also work as a form of self-enhancement. That is a type of motivation that serves to self-protect in order to maintain self-esteem. Sedikides uses the term self-enhancement and defines it as the interest that an individual has in advancing one or more self-domains or defending against negative self-views. One can argue that these motivational constructs can have importance in maintaining psychological and physical well-being in conditions like ABI, where a person is at risk of failure or experiencing damage to their self-esteem. There are a variety of strategies that people can use to enhance their sense of personal worth. For example, they can downplay skills that they lack, or they can criticize others in order to make themselves seem better by comparison. These strategies are successful to the extent that people tend to think of themselves as having more positive qualities and fewer negative qualities compared to others. People with low self-esteem use more indirect strategies, for example by avoiding situations in which their negative qualities will be noticeable or downplaying their importance.

Hope versus despair – the risk of demoralization

Hope is created by discovering a desired future and taking steps toward it. Its counterpart, despair, can be understood as the complete loss or absence of hope. For adults with ABI, despair can pose a greater threat to survival than the disease itself.

Demoralization was originally proposed by Jerome Frank, who described it as the state of mind of a person deprived of spirit or courage, disheartened, bewildered, and thrown into disorder or confusion (Frank, 1974; Frank & Frank 1991). Frank proposed that this state of mind occurs in many persons who seek support, regardless of their diagnostic label (Frank & Frank, 1991). In addition, demoralization always takes place within the context of a past, present, anticipated, or imagined stressful situation. To further characterize the concept of demoralization, it has been proposed that demoralization is subjective incompetence (SI) and that demoralization involves both SI and symptoms of distress, such as depression, anxiety, resentment, anger, or combinations thereof (Frank & Frank, 1991). SI is understood as a self-perceived incapacity to perform tasks and express feelings considered appropriate in a stressful situation, resulting in pervasive uncertainty and doubt about the future. The stressful situation disconfirms assumptions about self and others and about the continuity of the past and present with the future. Individuals with SI are uncertain, facing a dilemma, unclear as to ways out of the situation, etc. Demoralization is often accompanied with distress.

Distress has been very broadly defined as:

> a multifactorial, unpleasant, emotional experience of a psychological (cognitive, behavioral, emotional), social and/or spiritual nature that may interfere with the ability to cope effectively, its physical symptoms and its treatment and that extends along a continuum, ranging from common normal feelings of vulnerability, sadness, and fears to problems that can become disabling, such as depression, anxiety, panic, social isolation, and existential and spiritual crisis.
>
> (McFarland & Holland, 2016, p. 999)

SI and distress co-occur when perceived stress is high and/or social support is weak. The combination of SI with depression or other forms of nonspecific or specific distress constitutes demoralization (de Figueiredo & Frank, 1982; de Figueiredo, 2012).

As the intensity or duration of the stressful situation increases, SI eventually becomes helplessness. This happens when a person feels that they are unable to have an impact on the outcome of a situation, regardless of whether that outcome is good or bad, but they still *hope* that the circumstances will change. In some cases, an individual who is helpless eventually also becomes hopeless, that is, certain that a positive outcome will not take place or that a negative outcome will take place.

In the following interview, Eric show signs of hopelessness by internalizing the narratives of the professionals:

E: … because when you go through something like this, right, then it feels like a lot of failures, where you get this wet cloth in your face all the time because you hear, "Well this you cannot do," and "This you cannot do," and "This is not possible," and "This you'll never be able to do again," and …

I: Yes. When you refer to it as "hell" is that because this is the worst thing that could happen ever? This is the ultimate worst thing?

E: Yes, I think so. Because there are so many time points where the only thing you can do is just to sit and wait, where you … where I feel that I have to sit down and say to myself: "Okay, you cannot do bloody nothing. You can sit down and wait," and that is not very pleasant. Another thing is when I sit and watch TV and see nature or sports programs – for example, climbing mountains and running […] Then I have to say to myself: This you'll never be able to do again.

(Eric, 2015, research interview)

This cascade of events, which in this example made Eric feel increasingly disabled, culminate in feelings of existential despair and meaninglessness – or in some cases attempts of suicide. As noted by Abramson, Metalsky, and Alloy (1989), hopelessness always involves helplessness, i.e., hopelessness is a subset of helplessness, and therefore, when hopelessness occurs, helplessness also occurs.

Hopelessness is a mental state that is distinct from depression (Glanz, Haas, & Sweeney, 1995; Shahar, Bareket, Rudd, & Joiner, 2006). When measured with the Beck Hopelessness Scale, hopelessness has been shown in psychiatric patients to be a stronger predictor of suicide than depression (Wetzel, Margulies, & Davis, 1980; Beck, Steer, Beck, & Newman, 1993). In addition, hopelessness is associated with demoralization, impaired well-being, and poor quality of life (e.g. Sullivan, 2003).

Agency versus helplessness

Agency can be understood from a discursive viewpoint as the subject's ability to become a co-creator or a co-deconstructionist of a discourse. Even though we do not talk about a stable self, personality traits, or something internal within a discursive psychological approach, I still see distinctions between the interviewed adults with ABI with regard to the extent to which they took up positions and accepted the labels, and the narratives that were offered to them. Some participants seemed to be highly agentive and had strong views about not being disabled. Agency is acting in the expectation that one's actions can make a meaningful difference. Helplessness is acting – or not acting – with the expectation that one's actions make no difference. Often illnesses erode a sense of agency. However, there is *never* a time when *nothing* can be done. Thus, we need to ask reflective questions that help a person to mobilize and encourage a sense of agency and hope in them.

References

Abramson, L. Y., Metalsky, G. I., & Alloy, L. B. (1989). Hopelessness depression: A theory – based sub-type of depression. *Psychological Review*, 96(2), 358–372.
Beck, A. T., Steer, R. A., Beck, J. S., & Newman, C. F. (1993). Hopelessness, depression, suicidal ideation, and clinical diagnosis of depression. *Suicide Life-Threat*, 23(2), 139–145.

de Figueiredo, J. M. & Frank, J. D. (1982). Subjective incompetence, the clinical hallmark of demoralization. *Comprehensive Psychiatry*, 23(4), 353–363.

de Figueiredo, J. M. (2012). Deconstructing demoralization: Subjective incompetence and distress in the face of adversity. In R. D. Alarcon & J. B. Frank (Eds.). *The psychotherapy of hope: The legacy of persuasion and healing* (pp. 107–124). Baltimore, MD: The Johns Hopkins University Press.

Frank, J. D. & Frank, J. B. (1991). *Persuasion and healing: A Comparative study of psychotherapy*. Baltimore, MD: Johns Hopkins University Press.

Frank, J. D. (1974). Psychotherapy: the restoration of morale. *American Journal of Psychiatry*, 131(3), 271–274.

Glanz, L. M., Haas, G. L., & Sweeney, J. A. (1995). Assessment of hopelessness in suicidal patients. *Clinical Psychological Review*, 15(1), 49–64.

Hagger, B. F. (2011). *An exploration of self-disclosure after traumatic brain injury*. Ph.D. thesis submitted to the University of Birmingham, UK, for the degree of Doctor of Philosophy. Unpublished manuscript.

McFarland, D. C. & Holland, J. C. (2016). The management of psychological issues in oncology. *Clinical Advances Hematology Oncology*, 14(12), 999–1009.

Mead, G. H. (1913). The social self. *Journal of Philosophy, Psychology and Scientific Methods*, 10(12), 374–380.

Rollnick, S., Miller, W. R., & Butler, C. C. (2013). *Motivationssamtalen i sundhedssektoren*. Copenhagen, Denmark: Hans Reitzels Forlag.

Sedikides, C. & Gregg, A. P. (2008). Self-enhancement: Food for thought. *Perspectives on Psychological Science*, 3(2), 102–116.

Shahar, G., Bareket, L., Rudd, M. D., & Joiner, T. E. (2006). In severely suicidal young adults, hopelessness, depressive symptoms, and suicidal ideation constitute a single syndrome. *Psychological Medicine*, 36(7), 913–922.

Sullivan, M. D. (2003). Hope and hopelessness at the end of life. *American Journal Geriatric Psychiatry*, 11(4), 393–405.

Wetzel, R-D., Margulies, T., & Davis, R. (1980). Hopelessness, depression, and suicide intent. *Journal of Clinical Psychiatry*, 41(5), 159–160.

9 Personal competencies and resilience

Rehabilitation originates from a biomedical field (the medical model) where identification of pathology was seen as a first step to problem-solving. However, the bio–psycho–social model and research in resilience has challenged and developed this concept. In addition to focusing on what goes wrong with people who become chronically symptomatic and function poorly after adversity, we have begun to question what goes right in people who negotiate potentially traumatic events with equanimity. What are the natural mechanisms that allow most people to cope successfully with adversity? What are they doing and how are they coping?

> *You see a lot of different types at the rehabilitation center, who each have their own approach to life. I have thought a lot about why some people so quickly become chronic in their condition, while others don't, and I have come to the conclusion that it has to do with what you have with you in your backpack, what you have seen through life, that you have a strong will to do things every day – what we do in our life is about will. We talk way too little about personal competences and how to work with them and develop them. Where do we get our identity from? There can be several generations on social welfare in your family and it can be those patterns you narrate yourself from.*
>
> (Lillian, 2014, research interview)

This quote illustrates the importance of exploring personal competencies and different ways of coping with trauma as part of the rehabilitation process. Problems and life transitions, such as acquired brain injury (ABI), are handled quite differently across individuals during the rehabilitation process. Therefore, the focus must be not only on pathologies, but also on personal competencies, without making them an individual problem or responsibility. The focus should not only be on the fact that the individual has deficits, which are internalized into a new self-perception and identity, but also on how to strengthen personal skills for handling difficult life transitions, and how this happens in social settings and in interaction with others. To this end, the concept of resilience is useful, and this chapter aims to introduce the concept, presenting an ABI resilience model as a contribution to existing rehabilitation practice.

In the study of resilient outcomes in adults, there have been approaches that have suffered from serious conceptual misunderstandings, e.g. treating resilience as a personality characteristic, as the absence of symptoms and full recovery, or as a general term to connote average levels of psychological adjustment. For instance, personality rarely explains more than a small portion of the actual variance in people's behavior across situations. Thus, the notion of a resilient type at best addresses only a small piece of the overall puzzle of determining who will or will not be resilient. Resilience can be summarized as a mix of several factors: (1) personal competencies such as optimism and the ability to adapt; (2) psychosocial factors in an individual's family; and (3) context-based factors such as a supportive school, workplace, etc.

The study of resilience in individuals with ABI is in its infancy, but initial results already suggest that resilience contributes to positive rehabilitation outcomes (Bertisch, Rath, Long, Ashman, & Rashid, 2014). Research has indicated that most people who experience a traumatic event are resilient and "bounce back," even though initially they may catastrophize when predicting their emotional reactions (Gilbert, Morewedge, Risen, & Wilson, 2004). In general, people are poor at predicting how long their emotional reactions will last: overprediction of distress is generally matched by a faster-than-anticipated return to baseline functioning. Although this response pattern has been documented in individuals without cognitive impairment (Gilbert et al., 2004), it has not been adequately examined among people with cognitive and emotional changes secondary to a neurologic injury, such as ABI.

Every ABI is unique: even though two individuals may suffer from the same type of brain injury, this traumatic event will have individual consequences and they will adjust and cope with it in different ways. Based on interviews with adults, a colleague and I developed the ABI resilience model (Larsen & Glintborg, 2018). This model is a further development of Herman et al.'s resilience model (Herman et al., 2011, p. 261), which presents an overview of factors that enhance or reduce homeostasis or resilience (see Figure 9.1).

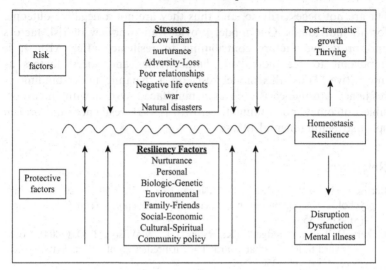

Figure 9.1 Factors that enhance or reduce homeostasis or resilience
Source: Herman et al., 2011, p. 262. With permission.

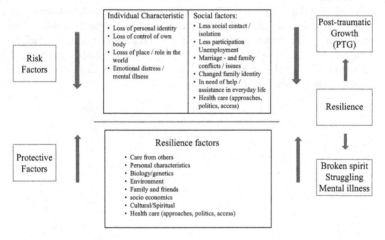

Figure 9.2 ABI resilience model
Source: Larsen and Glintborg, 2018.

In our model (Figure 9.2), we have changed the "outcome" boxes (the three boxes on the right side). "Thriving" and "Homeostasis" have been integrated into "Resilience," and "Disruption" and "Dysfunction" have been exchanged for "Broken spirit" and "Struggling," because disabilities can potentially be a stress factor, but are not necessarily so, and thus they are not a negative outcome for all individuals. Our model provides an overview of risk factors and protective factors contributing to resilience after ABI. It is important to see individual characteristics and social factors as interactive. Thus, this model rests on a dynamic understanding of resilience. Resilience is seen as a multifaced system with three possible outcomes: post-traumatic growth (PTG), resilience, and broken spirit/struggling/mental illness.

References

Bertisch, H., Rath, J., Long, C., Ashman, T., & Rashid, T. (2014). Positive psychology in rehabilitation medicine: A brief report. *NeuroRehabilitation*, 34(3), 573–585.

Gilbert, D. T., Morewedge, C. K., Risen, J. L., & Wilson, T. D. (2004). Looking forward to looking backward: The misprediction of regret. *Psychological Science*, 15(5), 346–350.

Herrman, H., Stewart, D. E., Diaz-Granados, N., Berger, E. L., Jackson, B., & Yuen, T. (2011). What is resilience? *The Canadian Journal of Psychiatry*, 56 (5), 258–265.

Larsen, K. & Glintborg, C. (2018). Resiliens og identitetsrekonstruktion hos unge med senhjerneskader [Resilience and identity reconstruction in adolescents with late brain damage]. In C. Glintborg (Ed.), *Rehabiliteringspsykologi: en introduktion i teori og praksis* [*Rehabilitation psychology – an introduction to theory and clinical practice*] (pp. 193–218). Aarhus, Denmark: Aarhus University Press.

10 Shame and self-criticism

ABI survivors are considerably more likely to suffer from depression, anxiety, and post-traumatic stress disorder (PTSD), and they are at a higher risk of committing suicide than those in the general population (see, for example, Hesdorffer, Rausch, & Tamminga, 2009). The brain injury can present psychological difficulties for the survivors. For some it is a new experience, for others it exacerbates pre-existing difficulties.

Over recent decades there has been an increasing awareness of shame-based syndromes (Kaufman, 1989). Examples of shame-based syndromes are drug and substance abuse and eating disorders. In such clinical conditions, the feeling of shame is often both a cause and a consequence. Emotional difficulties following acquired brain injury (ABI) are related to or result from the life-changing ABI. These consequences may be underpinned and maintained by severe self-criticism and shame alongside an inability to self-soothe. Shame can also have a great impact on the identity formation process.

Wurmser (1981) describes in his book, *The Mask of Shame*, how shame can be masked by and integrated into emotional expression and behavior. He describes this mask of shame/defense as "screen effects." Examples of these screen effects can be *grandiose behavior* where the individual can cling to fantasies about his or her greatness. In my research, I also found examples of this, for example in narratives about returning to work and the ability to do so. Even though some participants had been advised to take a flexible or part-time job, some created narratives on how they would go from being a part-time telephone salesperson to becoming the director of the department in no time.

This form of masking can also result from depression, particularly when an individual feels very downhearted because of guilt or loss. Entering rehabilitation can also be shameful. Seeking help from others can itself feel shameful, resulting in further shame.

In my research, I found different elements of shame. In the following quote we meet Tina who used to run marathons, worked abroad as a butcher, and in general was a very active and confident person. She described how her ABI, and the rehabilitation process that followed, impacted her self-confidence and identity:

> *I'm not the same person – my self-confidence has changed ... What I used to be great at doing, I can't do anymore.*
>
> (Tina, 2017, research interview)

After the injury, Tina had to give up her job as a butcher. However, two years post-injury she had an internship in a butchery as part of her vocational rehabilitation. She described this new situation as shameful. *"I used to have others in apprenticeship, but now the roles have shifted."* Her mentor at the butchery was younger than she was and was in fact a butcher she knew before she had the injury, only at that time she has been the more experienced one.

Stanley explains how shameful it was to recognize that the task the neuropsychologist gave him was a mathematical task his son could do, but that he, Stanley, was not able to solve.

> *It was terrible because it was so hard. I knew that the tasks were simple, however they were still incredibly difficult for me to solve. After half-an-hour, I finally finished the task but was overwhelmed with hopelessness and despair and started to cry in front of the neuropsychologist and again when I was alone in the afternoon. It was a surreal experience. Will I ever be able to help my children with their homework?*
>
> (Stanley, 2017, research interview)

During my fieldwork, I observed assessment sessions between clients and neuropsychologists. Here, I also observed how clients became affected emotionally during these testing situations (e.g. crying); however, their emotional states and reactions, which were caused by the assessments, as in Stanley's case, were not addressed. Clearly, the focus here was on assessing cognitive functioning.

Also, relatives identified shame and guilt in their partners:

> *I often cry. Mostly when I'm alone and to myself. I do not know who to go to or what to say. A couple of times, I have expressed my powerlessness to Stanley. He gets so overwhelmed with guilt, so the*

roles quickly shift again and I comfort him instead and put my own
tears and emotions away.

(Eve, 2017, research interview)

Eve's confession shows an imbalance in the relationship between her husband and herself, and a shift in their identities. Before Eve's husband, Stanley, suffered from ABI he was her "steady rock" and the one she could turn to. However, the ABI changed this. For several years after Stanley's ABI, the roles shifted and Eve had to become "the steady rock" of the family. Eve told me that she missed her husband as the one she could turn to, and she gave the above example of how, five years post-injury, she again tries to position Stanley as her "steady rock," but when she does, Stanley turns her suffering inwards on himself as shame and guilt. Stanley's shame and guilt, resulting from his ABI, keep this couple in distress and they struggle with non-preferred identities.

Shame was also present in relation to families with children. Some participants experienced that their children no longer related to them in the same way as they did pre-injury, e.g. the children would now primarily talk about school or more in-depth things with the healthy parent. This could initially be out of concern for the parent with ABI, or because that parent is simply too affected by their ABI to be able to take part in taking care of the children. However, for some families this grows into a habit where the healthy parent takes over many functions in the family, which again challenges the family's identity. For the individual with ABI, it can be shameful and hard to accept, ultimately causing them emotional distress. Thus, shame and self-criticism are strongly related to identity (re)construction after ABI. However, shame aspects of ABI are not addressed as part of current neurorehabilitation.

In contrast to the socially-distancing and isolating effects of shame, compassion tends to evoke more flexible ways of responding. It includes behavioral repertoires around caring for and relating to one's self and others that are associated with affiliative emotions such as warmth, interest, sympathetic joy, and pride. Shame that is shared can be converted into a shared sense of grief. As such, this chapter also briefly addresses clinical interventions targeting shame and self-criticism by focusing on how self-compassion can be adopted by people with ABI and their close relatives.

Research into the emotional experiences of ABI survivors has indicated that both internal and external shame and self-criticism form part of their emotional experience and are related to significant distress (Freeman, Adams, & Ashworth, 2014; Hagger, 2011; Jones & Morris, 2013).

An important contributor to shame and self-criticism is the societal devaluation of stigmatized identities. Shame is the emotional core of the experience of stigma and tends to involve fusion with beliefs of being flawed or unlovable. Self-stigma happens when you take on a socially devalued position. As the main emotional component of stigma, shame impedes social engagement, promotes interpersonal disconnection, and interferes with interpersonal problem-solving. The ashamed person's perspective is narrow and focused inward toward thoughts of a "bad self." Therefore, like other clinical populations, it is possible that these processes have a role in the development and maintenance of common psychological difficulties, such as anxiety and depression, in survivors of brain injury.

Compassion Focused Therapy

Shame is an experience that is not commonly discussed or described as central to many therapies or to neurorehabilitation. Shame is a subjective affective experience, seen as a response to how the self is negatively perceived/evaluated in the real (or imagined) mind of the self or the other (Goss, Gilbert, & Allan, 1994). Shame plays a central role in Compassion Focused Therapy (CFT) (Gilbert, 2002); it is linked to the fact that, as humans, we want to create positive feelings about ourselves in the minds of others (Gilbert, 2007). If we are sensitive to negative feelings and thoughts about ourselves in the minds of others, we can be vulnerable to external shame (Gilbert, 1997; 1998). Thus, if we experience our own self in the mind of another as rejected, unworthy, or vulnerable, this can make the social world unsafe. With internal shame our focus, or our attention, is inwardly on the negative evaluation of our own self as inadequate or flawed in our own mind.

CFT was developed to address shame and self-criticism and to foster the ability to self-soothe. More recently, Gracey and colleagues (Gracey, Evans, & Malley, 2009; Gracey & Ownsworth, 2011) have attempted to develop an evidence-based model that draws on a large body of research about the process of emotional adjustment post-injury. This model highlights a chain of processes connecting negative experiences of the self in valued pre-injury social and activity contexts to the internal development of self-discrepancies. These self-discrepancies are appraised as threatening and result in emotionally driven coping responses that, in conjunction with acquired deficits, conspire to generate further negative experiences in social and activity contexts post-injury. An approach to holistic rehabilitation that systematically addresses components of this model has been described, but not evaluated (Gracey & Ownsworth, 2011; Wilson & Gracey, 2009).

The three regulation systems in CFT

CFT suggests that the way we think and feel about ourselves and others is linked into three different types of regulation systems that have been highlighted in neuroscience research on emotion (Depue & Morrone-Strupinsky, 2005). The first of these is the threat system, which evolved to detect threat and instigate defensive/protective actions. It is associated with defensive emotions, such as anger and anxiety, and defensive behaviors, such as fight, flight, submit, and freeze responses. The threat system narrows attention and can focus the mind on threat. The neurophysiology of the threat system, and how it regulates emotional, cognitive, and behavioral processes, is increasingly well understood (LeDoux, 1998).

The second major regulation system is focused on acquiring resources. All living things need to be motivated to secure the resources required for their survival and reproduction. This system is especially associated with dopaminergic drive and motivational systems, which are energizing (Depue & Morrone-Strupinsky, 2005).

The third regulation system is linked to contentment and being neither threatened nor driven to succeed. These states are associated with quiescence (Depue & Morrone-Strupinsky, 2005). Fundamental to CFT is research that shows this system is linked to a sense of "peaceful well-being," and it is often referred to as the "soothing–contentment system." This system seems to be particularly involved with the attachment/affiliative system and is partly regulated through the endorphins and oxytocin hormone (Carter, 2014; MacDonald & MacDonald, 2010). The evolution of attachment and affiliation as an affect and drive regulator has had a fundamental influence on the evolution of the mammalian brain, the autonomic nervous system, the emergence of social intelligence, and affect regulation (Bjorklund, 1997; Mikulincer & Shaver, 2007; Porges, 2007). Research also indicates that oxytocin has a direct influence on the amygdala and reduction in the perception of threat (Kirsch et al., 2005).

CFT offers a novel and compelling way of conceptualizing psychological difficulties after brain injury. In particular, given that CFT incorporates neuroscientific and neurophysiological factors into its model of affect regulation, it translates usefully for those with ABI where neurological damage is likely to affect such systems. As one participant stated, *"I had a tricky brain before my brain injury, but now I have an even trickier one."* Thus, CFT with its adaptations to the neurobiological aspects of emotion regulation can facilitate the rationalization of emotional difficulties linked with the consequences of ABI, which can be lacking in other psychotherapeutic approaches.

Research in CFT and ABI

The concepts and clinical application of CFT have yet to be explored in depth with people who have ABI. It would be useful to investigate further the experience of shame and self-criticism in this population, in order to understand the nature of these emotional experiences and responses in relation to ABI. However, findings reveal that adults with ABI have described positively how CFT has helped them to relate to themselves in a new way and re-evaluate their sense of worth, as well as providing tools to manage their difficulties. A key part of this process was understanding and developing empathy for their own situations. They described how this allowed them to make changes to how they relate to others as well as to themselves. One clearly different and interesting aspect of the findings is that the survivors are able to take positively-learned knowledge from neuropsychology, which helps them not only to make sense of their "trickier brains," but also to see that this situation is "not their fault." The "tricky brain" concept is a key principle of CFT and is particularly salient for ABI populations where the tricky brain becomes even trickier given the impact that frontal lobe and other damage can have on executive control of emotions and rational thinking abilities. This added neuropsychological dimension to the tricky brain is a key part of CFT psycho-education.

References

Bjorklund, D. F. (1997). The role of immaturity in human development. *Psychological Bulletin*, 122(2), 153–169.

Carter, S. C. (2014). Oxytocin pathways and the evolution of human behavior. *Annual Review of Psychology*, 65(1), 17–39.

Depue, R. A. & Morrone-Strupinsky, J. V. (2005). A neurobehavioural model of affiliative bonding. *Behavioural and Brain Sciences*, 28(3), 313–395.

Freeman, A., Adams, M., & Ashworth, F. (2014). An exploration of the experience of self in the social world for men following traumatic brain injury. *Neuropsychological Rehabilitation*, 25(2), 189–215.

Gilbert, P. (1997). The evolution of social attractiveness and its role in shame, humiliation, guilt and therapy. *British Journal of Medical Psychology*, 70(2), 113–147.

Gilbert, P. (1998). The evolved basis and adaptive functions of cognitive distortions. *British Journal of Medical Psychology*, 71(4), 447–464.

Gilbert, P. (2002). Evolutionary approaches to psychopathology and cognitive therapy. Special Edition: Evolutionary psychology and cognitive therapy, *Journal of Cognitive Psychotherapy: An International Quarterly*, 16(3), 263–294.

Gilbert, P. (2007). The evolution of shame as a marker of relationship security. In J. L. Tracey, R. W., Robins, & J. P. Tangney (Eds.), *The self-conscious emotions: Theory and research* (pp. 283–309). New York: Guilford Press.

Goss, K., Gilbert, P., & Allan, S. (1994). An exploration of shame measures, I: The other as shamer scale. *Personality and Individual Differences*, 17(5), 713–717.

Gracey, F., Evans, J. J., & Malley, D. (2009). Capturing process and outcome in complex rehabilitation interventions: A "Y-shaped" model. *Neuropsychological Rehabilitation*, 19(6), 1–24.

Gracey, F. & Ownsworth, T. (2011). The experience of self in the world: The personal and social contexts of identity change after brain injury. In J. Jetten, C. Haslam & A. Haslam (Eds.), *A social cure: Identity, health and well-being*. Hove, UK: Psychology Press.

Hagger, B. F. (2011). *An exploration of self-disclosure after traumatic brain injury*. Thesis submitted to the University of Birmingham, UK, for the degree of Doctor of Philosophy. Unpublished manuscript.

Hesdorffer, D. C., Rausch, S. L., & Tamminga, C. A. (2009). Long-term psychiatric outcomes following traumatic brain injury: A review of the literature. *Journal Head Trauma Rehabilitation*, 24(6), 452–459.

Jones, L. & Morris, R. (2013). Experiences of adult stroke survivors and their parent carers: A qualitative study. *Clinical Rehabilitation*, 27(3), 272–280.

Kaufman, G. (1989). *The psychology of shame: Theory and treatment of shame-based syndromes*. New York: Springer.

Kirsch, P., Esslinger, C., Chen, Q., Mier, D., Lis, S., Siddhanti, S., & Meyer-Lindenberg, A. (2005). Oxytocin modulates neural circuitry for social cognition and fear in humans. *Journal of Neuroscience*, 25(49), 11489–11493.

LeDoux, J. (1998). *The emotional brain*. London: Weidenfeld & Nicolson.

MacDonald, K. & MacDonald, T. M. (2010). The peptide that binds: A systematic review of oxytocin and its prosocial effects in humans. *Harvard Review of Psychiatry*, 18(1), 1–21.

Mikulincer, M. & Shaver, P. R. (2007). Boosting attachment security to promote mental health, prosocial values, and inter-group tolerance. *Psychological Inquiry*, 18(3), 139–156.

Porges, S. W. (2007). The polyvagal perspective. *Biological Psychology*, 74(2), 116–143.

Wilson, B. A. & Gracey, G. (2009). Towards a comprehensive model of neuropsychological rehabilitation. In B. A. Wilson, F. Gracey, J. E. Evans, & A. Bateman (Eds.), *Neuropsychological rehabilitation: Theories, models, therapy and outcome* (pp. 1–21). Cambridge, UK: Cambridge University Press.

Wurmser, L. (1981). *The masks of shame*. Baltimore:, MD: Johns Hopkins University Press.

11 The role of peer support groups in identity (re)construction after acquired brain injury

Peer support groups established on the basis of an illness are important, not only because the group members share the same illness. As one participant said: *"we spend time together because we like each other, not just because we have a brain injury"* (Glintborg, 2015). The fact that people spend time with others they like, and experience "we are in it together" forms security in the group. Persons with acquired brain injury (ABI) describe that this facilitates change by propagating feelings of being understood. Research indicates that living with ABI can lead to social isolation and social stigma (Boden-Albala, Litwak, Elkind, Rundek, & Sacco, 2005; Hagger, 2011; Morton & Wehman, 1995). Thus, we need to acknowledge the value of relating to other survivors, as a way of resisting cultural discourses about disability, and as a source of self-cohesion in the process of identity reconstruction (Salas, Casassus, Rowlands, & Pimm, 2018). Further studies also highlight the positive effects of group membership for ABI survivors (Haslam et al., 2008). With reference to the theoretical foundation of Compassion Focused Therapy, the development and experience of understanding, empathic validation, and affiliative relationships, specifically in relation to one's difficulty, are thought to be key to the development of an affiliative compassionate approach to oneself (Bates, 2005).

Peer support groups represent a setting that may help an adult with ABI to overcome identity challenges (Bellon, Sando, Crocker, Farnden, & Duras, 2017). Support groups consist of people with similar fates, i.e. people who have survived a sudden brain injury. One may distinguish between support groups and self-help groups on the basis of their leadership (Finlayson & Cho, 2011). While support groups are led by peers, the self-help groups involve a professional facilitator. There is not, however, a consensus regarding this distinction in the literature. The rationale for both types of groups overlap – they are supposed to provide knowledge and information that facilitate the management of a given illness and/or disability and offer social contact. Furthermore, through participation in such a group, the person is given an opportunity to exchange experiences and reflect upon his/her own situation in a different way, as the individual experiences are shared and compared in the group. Such processes can contribute to establishment of new and more meaningful cognitive strategies and representations and help the affected individual to rediscover the meaning of life. Shadden and Agan (2004) point out that informal support groups may provide an opportunity for renegotiation of identity through narratives and discourses arising in the support group where the group participants mirror their own situation in each other. This in turn can improve their quality of life and sense of self. The research that directly addresses the benefits and effect of support groups in ABI population is sparse, although some studies have been carried out (Bellon et al., 2017; Hibbard et al., 2002; Jones et al., 2012; Lexell, Alkhed, & Olsson, 2013; McLean, Jarus, Hubley, & Jongbloed, 2012; Schwartzberg, 1994). Although support groups are associated with several advantages (e.g. feeling of acceptance by others, validation of one's own problems, practical information, and help) (Bellon et al., 2017), it cannot be taken for granted that a participation in a support group is always beneficial. For instance, it has been pointed out that some participants may find it difficult to relate to the topics and issues discussed in a group or they may not feel like being in touch with other brain injured people (Lexell et al., 2013; McLean et al., 2012). Although a few studies focusing on brain injured people and support groups have touched upon identity as an issue (for example, Jones et al., 2012; Lexell et al., 2013), none of them have specifically examined the role of support groups in the process of identity (re)construction.

To further explore the role of peer support for those with ABI, Rytter, Jørgensen, Thomassen and I performed a study examining the role of peer support groups in post-injury identity reconstruction. The aim of the study was to increase our understanding of how the process of identity (re)construction is influenced by participation in such a group. The study therefore sought to answer the following question: What is the importance of the self-narratives that arise in peer support groups for identity (re)construction in survivors of ABI? The support groups in the study functioned without a professional involvement and facilitation. We interviewed participants in two support groups. The obtained self-narratives were analyzed using a discursive approach. The analysis focused on the identification of self-narratives that either had an encouraging or inhibitory effect on the identity (re)construction. To our knowledge, only one other study has used the discursive approach. This study investigated the role of traumatic brain injury and interactions with significant others for the process of identity (re)construction (Cloute, Mitchell, & Yates, 2008).

Methods

Focus group interviews were chosen to facilitate the creation of a collective context that would enable insight into the narratives that arise spontaneously in the support group. The social context of the focus group interviews contains both the record of the individual responses and understandings and the knowledge derived from the social interaction itself (e.g. how social processes lead to particular interpretations and thereby norms of the group) (Halkier, 2010). The use of focus groups enables an examination of more complex topics. At the same time the synergy in group interaction offers more in-depth information as the group participants can discuss each other's experiences from a perspective that is unfamiliar to the researcher (Halkier, 2010). Furthermore, focus groups were chosen as they represent an appropriate tool when working with respondents who suffer cognitive and emotional impairments (Carey, 2011), as is presently the case. The focus group creates an informal atmosphere, which facilitates contributions even from respondents who would otherwise tend to withdraw due to their impairments (Carey, 2011). Finally, focus groups enable insights into the participants in local group settings and community, which was of particular importance for this study. The focus groups each consisted of three to four persons. The number of participants in each focus group paralleled the number of participants in the existing groups (outside of this study) and was intended to enable sufficient time for contributions from each participant. The individual respondents were unknown to the authors prior to the interview.

Participants

The participants were seven adults with ABI who participated in two different support groups in two geographically distant locations (Jutland, western Denmark and Funen, central Denmark). The respondents were recruited through the Danish Association of Brain Injured and the respective Facebook groups. At the outset, potential respondents received a letter describing the study and the purpose of the interview. Respondents had to comply with the following inclusion criteria: (1) age 18–50 years (as this period of life is characterized by pursuing goals in career and private life alike); (2) the hospitalization was finished and testing for brain injury sequelae completed; (3)

respondents in the individual focus groups had to be familiar with each other; and (4) any diagnosed mental disease other than brain injury had to be disclosed (the authors did not wish to exclude persons with other diagnoses, but wanted to be informed about this). In the end, none of the participants suffered from any other mental diseases and they came from two already established support groups. All respondents signed a written consent prior to the interviews. The consent summarized the aim of the study, the respondent's rights during and after interview, information regarding anonymity and audiorecording of the interviews. See Table 11.1 for the individual characteristics of the study respondents.

Support group 1 (SG1)

SG1 started in December 2014 and the participants meet once per month. When they meet, they speak about everyday life and the challenges related to ABI. There are three women and one man. Kirsten, 45 years, lives with her partner and two children. She is educated within the service area, but receives a disability pension. Peter is in his 40s and had previously worked as a craftsman. He has suffered two strokes and is in the process of clarifying whether he qualifies for disability pension. He got divorced after his injury and now lives with his daughter. Lone, 42 years, lives together with her husband and five children, of whom one is also brain injured. She is educated in craftsmanship but receives a disability pension. Jette, 21 years, lives with her fiancé. She was in the middle of her studies when she suffered the stroke. She is also in the process of clarifying whether she can receive a disability pension. None of the group participants have visible impairments, but Lone wears sunglasses as she gets headaches in strong light.

Support group 2 (SG2)

SG2 started more than ten years ago. The participants meet every other week in a coffee bar. When they meet, they talk about everyday life. Furthermore, there are events (e.g. lectures) that they go to together from time to time. The group consists of three men. Jonas, 42 years, is single and lives alone. When he was 10 years old, he was in a traffic accident that caused a brain injury with physical and linguistic consequences. He now works as a mechanic. Patrick, 37 years, is single and lives alone. Originally, he was involved in a traffic accident but since then he has suffered multiple minor strokes throughout his live. He has a job with light duties in a shop. He takes responsibility for the

Table 11.1 Demographic and injury-related characteristics of the study participants

Support group	Name	Age	Civil status	Education/work	Brain injury	Chronicity	Participation in support group
1	Kirsten	45	Cohabitant and children	Disability pension	Traumatic brain injury (TBI)	3 years	3 months
	Peter	40-ties	Divorced and child	Under clarification for disability pension	Stroke	< 1 year	3 months
	Lone	42	Married and children	Disability pension	Stroke	5.5 years	3 months
	Jette	21	With fiancé	Under clarification for disability pension	Stroke	2 years	3 months
2	Patrick	37	Single	Light duty job	Stroke	multiple minor strokes throughout life	10 years
	Daniel	26	Single	Light duty job	Tumour	16 years	2–3 years
	Jonas	42	Single	Mechanic	TBI	32 years	2–3 years

support group. Daniel, 26 years, developed a brain tumor at 10 years old, the removal of which resulted in a brain injury. He works at a supermarket in a job with light duties. Patrick and Daniel have no visible impairments.

Data collection

The data were collected from the focus group interviews that were performed separately in each group. The entire session lasted a maximum of two hours with a break after approximately the first hour. The session took place in a private setting, i.e. at the home of one of the group participants. This contributed to a trusting and safe atmosphere and helped to ensure confidentiality. The session contained an introduction, the focus group interview, and a debriefing. The introduction opened the session and contained a summary of the project, the plan for the focus group interview (with an explanation that it is primarily the respondents that are talking to each other), and a presentation of the participants and authors. The respondents also got an opportunity to pose questions. The interviews in both support groups were carried out by the same people (authors CJ and MNRT). One of the authors acted as the interviewer and the other as an observer. The presentation by the participants and the entire interview were audiotaped (excluding the break). The interviewer was following an interview guide containing five broadly formulated, open questions (e.g. "What do you get out of being part of a support group?" and "Are there any changes from before the brain injury and the way you are now?"). This was to ensure that the discussions in the group would be relevant for the research question. Additionally, several follow-up questions were formulated with the purpose of aiding the discussion if it came to a halt or moved away from relevant topics. The interviewer strived to enable the discussions, while trying to avoid controlling them. The interviewer also strived to invite all respondents to contribute to the discussions. The observer took notes about the responses of both the respondents and the interviewer. If relevant, these notes were later incorporated into the analysis. The observer was also acting as a support to the interviewer, in case the situation demanded it. After the interview, debriefing took place. During the debriefing, the respondents were asked about how they felt during the interview; and the interviewer and observer aimed at ensuring that the respondents left the session with a positive mind-set.

Data analysis

The recorded material was transcribed by two unbiased transcribers. All personal characteristics were concealed during the transcription process. The transcription presented in the analysis section used citations from the interviews. The transcribers were also asked to note down their immediate thoughts while transcribing the interview. The transcription notation has been adapted as follows:

Italics: emphasis in the analysis;
(...): omitted parts of the transcript that were irrelevant for the analysis;
...: pauses in the speech;
(unclear?): unclear speech;
/: if interrupted in the speech;
huhhuhhuh: laughter.

In line with Brinkmann and Kvale (2005), the authors tried to report the information from the interviews as accurately as possible, with the help of clarifying questions during the interview. Likewise, the authors also aimed at keeping a high level of transparency in order to enable the reader to judge the validity and reliability of the analysis.

Results/analysis

The following sections contain the analysis of narratives from SG1 and SG2.

SG1

The group interaction has a good flow and both the interviewer and the observer remain relatively passive while the respondents are discussing among themselves. The interviewer and observer have the impression that the atmosphere during the interview is similar to that during the regular meetings of the group. It is therefore assumed that the narratives and discourses that take place during this interview are likely to offer insight into the role the support group plays for the identity (re)construction of the individual participants. In the following, there is a description of three central themes that are present in the interview and that are likely to have had an impact on identity (re)construction: (1) insufficiency, (2) dependency, and (3) encounters with others.

Insufficiency

During the interview all respondents use narratives indicating that they position themselves today as insufficient compared to their premorbid self-perception.

INTERVIEWER: Can you feel the changes now after [injury], this support group has not been functioning for very long, but after you have started it ...?

PETER: (...) I have the feeling that they [the friends] actually see me as the old one, *him who could manage everything, him who was always there* and helped and ... and all things, and I *just can't do that anymore* and instead of and ... yeah, use a lot of energy and ... have to tell ... that *one can't* and all this stuff, and to defend it, yeah it's easier to just push them away.

(SG1, research interview)

Peter points out that previously it was *him who could manage everything, him who was always there* compared to now when he *just can't do that anymore*. This indicates a large change from the past to the present and relates to ID 1 regarding the navigation between constancy and change in the perception of self over time (ID 1: constancy vs. change). Furthermore, Peter mentions *can't* several times, which may indicate his positioning as insufficient. It is possible that Peter is under the influence of a postmodernistic, societal discourse that requires individuals to manage well on all fronts. This is not possible for Peter anymore due to his ABI, which leaves him feeling incapable and helpless. Peter's narrative indicates that he distances himself from his own previous image by using *him* while the use of *I* indicates that he sees the injury as part of his own self. At the same time, he is challenged by the change and refuses to accept it, indicated by the use of *one* when he talks about the current situation. Peter has lived with the condition for less than a year and he is therefore likely still in the middle of an adaptation process. This may be the reason why he is finding it difficult to share his condition with his friends. Finally, it should be noted that Peter does not respond directly to the interviewer's question, but instead begins to talk about the changes that he has experienced after his injury. This indicates that these changes largely preoccupy Peter's mind and may well overshadow other themes.

Positioning as insufficient is also present regarding parenthood together with an altered identity as a parent. These changes are coupled with feelings of guilt.

KIRSTEN: And we have given them the sorrow that they have an injured parent, and so/

PETER: Yep, exactly, and then one would like to compensate for everything, in impossible ways, I mean, it's in impossible ways all the time.

KIRSTEN: I have my son from Tuesday to Wednesday, and on Tuesday, I buy all the stuff that I know he likes, and there's everything that he likes in the fridge ...

(SG1, research interview)

Peter confirms the narrative of Kirsten and to a degree completes her sentence, which indicates that, together, they construct the identity of an insufficient parent. Kirsten describes *we have given them the sorrow* because they now have an *injured parent*. Her use of *we* indicates that she not only positions herself as an insufficient parent, but positions all parents with ABI as insufficient. It is interesting that she uses the word *sorrow* as this is quite powerful and relates to the feeling of loss, the loss of the "old" mother now replaced by an injured mother. Peter continues stating that he therefore tries to compensate for this loss in *impossible ways* and that this is impossible for him. This may relate to the respondents' new values and priorities due to ABI, where the parent identity becomes the dominant identity since other identities, such as work identities, can no longer be maintained. It is possible that the premorbid parent identity had not been as perfect as it is currently described. In such a case, this impedes the identity (re)construction as the individual strives to achieve something that is impossible – even for a healthy parent. This is evident from the following conversation.

KIRSTEN: But do we necessarily have to be super mums and dads that we once dreamt about, *aren't we good enough as we are*, one way or another?

LONE: But that's what we've got to do, *we have no choice*.

KIRSTEN: Well, if we just tell our kids that we need some rest now, or at that time, and then just *move on from there*, instead of banging our heads, what do you think?

PETER: Yeah, but I think actually that we sometimes *that we ...*/

KIRSTEN: *We use a lot of energy* on that Peter.

PETER: Yes, exactly Kirsten, that we actually want to be more than we were before we became injured.

(SG1, research interview)

Kirsten asks *aren't we good enough as we are* indicating that she distances herself from the discourse regarding the perfect parent and instead constructs a positioning as a *good enough* parent. However, Kirsten also describes the sorrow she experiences toward her children, which illustrates the ambivalence with respect to her positioning as a good enough parent. It should also be noted that Kirsten presents her viewpoint as a question, which may indicate that she is trying to free herself from this societal discourse. Nevertheless, Lone answers *we have no choice* and rejects thereby Kirsten's suggestion and maintains her positioning as insufficient parent. Kirsten does not validate Lone's positioning and states that it is time to *move on from there*. It is possible that by doing so, Kirsten attempts to help Lone to see beyond her limitations and thereby she constructs her identity as a therapist. Peter seems to confirm Kirsten and Kirsten continues by saying *we use a lot of energy on that* whereby she tries to support Peter in him taking a distance from the discourse about the perfect parent.

It is evident that Lone positions herself as the one who is most severely affected in the group.

INTERVIEWER: (...) What do you get out of being part of such a [support group]?

LONE: (...) I could see how my kids they *suffered*, (...) [she gives a long description of the children's concrete reactions to Lone's injury].

KIRSTEN: *Jesus Christ, she talks* ... isn't it unbelievable? (...)

LONE: It was this thing with the kids, it's because I am so sorry about it, I am really sorry.

KIRSTEN: Yeah, *we are all very sorry about it*, I can feel that.

(SG1, research interview)

Lone points out how her children *suffered* due to her brain injury and gives a concrete description of their reactions. This indicates that she is very affected and feels guilty toward them, and that she is positioning herself as the one who is most severely affected. Kirsten interrupts her by saying *Jesus Christ, she talks* indicating that she thinks Lone has been talking too long while she wants to create space for herself and other respondents in the group. Afterward Kirsten says *we are all very sorry about it*, and by using *we* she indicates that she positions the whole group as parents who are burdened by the feeling of guilt toward their children. She thus rejects Lone's positioning herself as the only one who has that feeling. Additionally, it is also likely that Kirsten stops Lone in order to bring the conversation back to the question originally asked by the interviewer ("What do you get out of being part of such a group?"). Shortly after this, the interviewer restates the question.

INTERVIEWER: But are these things something you can talk about in this group?

PETER: Just the fact that you are *understood.*

LONE: *My daughter, she has moved out from home because of me...* and the circumstances ... it is only in this group ... *not even my family knows it.*

(SG1, research interview)

This excerpt illustrates again that Lone in particular is burdened by feeling guilty. Peter starts out trying to answer the interviewer's question, and states that he feels *understood* in the group. Lone is nevertheless finding it difficult to give up the previous topic and continues by saying *My daughter, she has moved out from home because of me.* It may be that Lone has overheard the interviewer's question, possibly because the previous topic was of great importance to her. At the same time, she conveys a powerful message and this may strengthen her position in the group as the one most affected. Moreover, her wording *because of me* witnesses that she sees herself as the sole reason for her daughter moving out, and that she has thereby failed as a parent. She goes on and adds *not even my family knows it,* which may mean that she is ashamed of not being the parent she would like to be as well as being ashamed of her injury. It indicates that there is a deep confidentiality in the group enabling conversation about emotional matters and even matters that are otherwise taboo.

The respondents thus have several narratives that point at their insufficiency. On the other hand, there are also narratives that indicate that the brain injury has also been associated with new values and more valuable identities. At the end of the interview, the interviewer asks:

INTERVIEWER: Is there anything now, at the very end, that you think we should know?

(...)

JETTE: In any case, one has to *learn to value everything* one can do.

PETER: Yes.

KIRSTEN: Yes, that is true.

JETTE: No matter how annoying it is/

KIRSTEN: Well, there are also some good things, I don't know, I mean that we've also begun to have other values in life.

JETTE: Yes, that's right.

PETER: Yeah, for sure.

INTERVIEWER: What could that be, for example?

PETER: Well, I'd say that I ... *am much more in touch with myself emotionally, much more ... just that/*

KIRSTEN: *To learn about yourself.*

PETER: Yes, and to be able to *cry* ... I haven't ... I guess I've never tried it before, that's right, I haven't ... from the time I was a kid, looking around, I haven't *cried* one single time ... Now I've learned it, dammit, I've got to recognize that ... just the fact that you *dare and ... get in touch with yourself, with your inner world, I haven't dared before,* and I am glad that I do today, yeah, one way or another, I am actually grateful for that ... yeah.

KIRSTEN: Yeah, one can even start *crying* when seeing the daffodil getting above the ground, or the waves hitting the beach, or something else like that.

PETER: Yes, or that there is one or another sweet cartoon that one watches with one's daughter and then I think, Jesus Christ, what a *crybaby* ... /

KIRSTEN: Or at home, when someone does something nice for someone else, one becomes quite *moved*, Jesus, such nice people.

PETER: It is indeed so.

(SG1, research interview)

This excerpt indicates that there is a consensus in the group regarding the redefinition of values after the injury. At the beginning, Jette stated that they *learn to value everything*, which is confirmed by both Peter and Kirsten. Peter describes *dare and ... get in touch with yourself, with your inner world, I haven't dared before,* which indicates that he is constructing an identity as a man that is today able to get in contact with his feelings. Interestingly, in the interaction between Peter and Kirsten, Peter states that ... *am much more in touch with myself emotionally, much more ... just that/* after which Kirsten completes his sentence saying *to learn about yourself.* Thereby, she overtakes Peters narrative, which indicates that they together construct a more emotional identity. This is emphasized by their choice of words like *cry, crying, crybaby.* The interaction between the respondents indicates that the support group supports the individuals in the group in redefining the values, which enables them to construct more valuable identities.

Dependency

Another dominant identity construction that is obvious from the interview is the positioning of the respondents as dependent on others.

KIRSTEN: (...) live together with my cohabitant [gives his name] who is an *old man*, but *he is good with me*, and *that is what matters, isn't it* ...

(SG1, research interview)

Kirsten's description of her cohabitant as an *old man* and the wording *that is what matters, isn't it* may mean that she thinks that she has to "make do with" her partner after her ABI. She describes *he is good with me*, which indicates that she positions herself as dependent on her cohabitant who is a caregiver for her. It is possible that her thinking about a partner has changed after her injury and the most important thing now is that her partner *is good with her* and accepts her as she is.

The other respondents also present narratives that indicate dependency.

INTERVIEWER: But does it mean anything for you in general, this thing about what other people think?

(...)

KIRSTEN: *But isn't it the same for you* that those people that actually take good care of one, help one along the way, and that kind of thing ... that one then goes around and feels this endless gratitude and one feels that you've got to be grateful for them being the way they are, or for what they have done for you ... (unclear?), *I really feel that I've got to be thankful from now on and for the rest of my time.*

PETER: Yes, but I find it *degrading*.

JETTE: [toward Kirsten] That's the thing you wrote on Facebook, I could just *recognize* that ... but yes, that's true.

KIRSTEN: Yeah, yeah.

PETER: Each and every time I get help, well, then I feel it's *degrading*, because that reminds me that can't do it myself ... and that annoys me, so *that's why I want to do everything myself* (...).

(SG1, research interview)

Kirsten states *I really feel that I've got to be thankful from now on and for the rest of my time,* which illustrates that she is in debt toward her relatives/caregivers since she is dependent on them and cannot contribute the same way as before. She starts by *But isn't it the same for you* whereby she creates a question for the entire group. It is possible that she seeks the group's confirmation regarding the "small-d" discourse about endless gratitude and dependency on others. Jette validates Kirsten's discourse by stating that she *recognizes* it with respect to her own life. Peter, on the one hand, validates Kirsten's positioning as grateful and on the other, adds that he finds it *degrading,* thereby showing ambivalence in his narrative. His choice of the word *degrading,* as well as his repeated use of it, is quite strong and indicates that he is distancing himself from the positioning as dependent. Eventually he demonstratively proclaims *that's why I want to do everything myself.* This small-d discourse present in the conversation regarding dependency on others may lead to feelings of guilt and incapability toward their surroundings in some respondents. Peter, in contrast, constructs a narrative that shows agency, where he rejects being dependent on others. Failure to recognize and accept the limitations of his condition may, however, inhibit his identity (re)construction.

Positioning as dependent is also prevalent with respect to the public sector. In Denmark, it is the local municipalities that are in charge of retraining and rehabilitation after hospital discharge. Municipalities are supposed to provide service, support, and aids across the needs and legislative domains (health, social, employment, education, etc.).

As a response to the interviewer's question regarding what do the respondents get out of participation in a support group, a longer discussion gets started and Kirsten states:

(...)

KIRSTEN: It is a stressful system to get through, we also need to talk about that, from time to time, I think.

(SG1, research interview)

Kirsten describes a discourse where the system is *stressful.* This is a negatively charged expression whereby she positions herself as dissatisfied with the system. At the same time, she uses the pronoun *we,* which illustrates that she positions the whole group as dissatisfied with the system. Interestingly, the respondents present these narratives independently of interviewer's questions.

INTERVIEWER: (...) how does it work in general [your support group], do you have some events from time to time, or is it that you primarily take a cup coffee together and talk?

(...)

KIRSTEN: well, *nobody comes to you and tell you* that now, you can apply for such and such help, because that's what you apparently need ...
PETER: *Nope, the municipality is just silent.*
KIRSTEN: One has to *know everything*, what can you apply for, or figure out information about it, in any case.

(SG1, research interview)

In the excerpt, Kirsten says *nobody comes to you and tell you*, which indicates that she feels that she does not get sufficient support from the municipality. Peter accepts Kirsten's positioning of the municipality services as being unsatisfactory by stating *Nope, the municipality is just silent.* Kirsten adds to her explanation when she points out that the individual person is supposed to *know everything*, which further emphasizes the positioning of the municipality as unsatisfactory as it is the municipality and not the brain injured individual who should *know everything*. It is possible that Kirsten choses strategically to further elaborate on her description after Peter has validated her narrative. It is problematic that the respondents experience both dependency and stress in relation to the municipal services, as they have to use a lot of time and resources to figure out how the system actually works. This can position them as more passive. On the other hand, the information and experience exchange in the support group can facilitate the construction of agency.

PETER: (...) and it is as if *one's got to be down on one's knees and kiss their smelly feet*, isn't it, in order to, well, what a great help you have been to me, despite this not being any help at all ... I find it terribly degrading, because it is as if *they think that we just don't feel like it*, that is the attitude they show, and there's nothing I'd wish more than to go out and *take a full-time job and function normally* ... it is, I don't know where they have this ... this idea from (...) that now you are a little sick and that's why you don't want to do anything ... this is just not the case.

(SG1, research interview)

Peter illustrates symbolically how it feels: *one's got to be down on one's knees and kiss their smelly feet*, which again emphasizes his dissatisfaction with the municipal services. Moreover, he expresses that the municipality employees *think that we just don't feel like it*, which points at a discourse in the municipality where people with ABI are perceived as lazy and indolent. This indicates that Peter's narrative is influenced by a "them vs. us" discourse, where the municipal employees are positioned as being very different from people with ABI. It is possible that these strong narratives can impose a feeling of powerlessness regarding the management of their condition. The municipal assistance is essential in several aspects, for example regarding treatment, requalification, or the possibility of qualifying for disability pension. However, Peter's description also contains elements of him rejecting this discourse, and instead he adopts an identity as a person with agency by stating that he most of all wishes to *take a full-time job and function normally.*

Respondents also spontaneously express that they need help from a psychologist with regard to their ABI. There is a longer discussion about becoming at ease with the consequences of a brain injury and Peter describes his hospitalization:

PETER: Psychologically, I began to go down, slowly but steadily.
KIRSTEN: Yes, *because nobody takes care of that at all.*
PETER: Not the least little bit, and that, and *I kept on asking, if it wasn't possible.*

(SG1, research interview)

Peter's and Kirsten's narratives witness that they had felt alone regarding the mental and psychological consequences of their brain injuries. It is noteworthy that Kirsten states *because nobody takes care of that at all.* Her narrative is influenced by the "us vs. them" discourse, where she positions herself, and potentially all people with ABI, as being markedly different from professionals that take care of them in the public sector. Peter validates the discourse and expresses *I kept on asking, if it wasn't possible.* His narrative is likely to be influenced by the "Capital-D" medical discourse where it is the physician that approves whether a person is sick or not. He underscores this by *I kept on asking,* which indicates that he did not experience any involvement or understanding when it came to the help he has been offered. This may have left him in a more passive position. The interviewer poses an additional question to get more insight into the issue:

INTERVIEWER: What do you actually think about the offers and services that are available, now you have started this group on your own, but how about other offers?

JETTE: Well, the psychologist services, I think, that should be a must, I mean *one should not even have to ask, because that is what we all need so badly.*

LONE: I agree, and I think it's not only us, but also what our *relatives* need ... 'cause our (unclear?) partners and kids ...

(SG1, research interview)

Jette says that, regarding a psychologist, *one should not even have to ask, because that is what we all need so badly* whereby she criticizes the availability of psychologist services as they should be something that one is offered as a minimum requirement after surviving brain injury. Lone confirms her position and also adds that relatives are in need of that type of service. It is interesting that Lone chooses to include the relatives, which may indicate that she feels guilty toward them. It is possible that the discourse regarding everybody needing help from a psychologist may have an inhibitory effect on identity reconstruction. By experiencing that the need is not met, the respondents are left more passive. On the other hand, the narratives in the group also indicate that the support group can compensate for this lack of professional assistance, at least to a degree.

JETTE: At ... yeah, there are things where we can *help each other to move on*, also with the everyday things, so it is not just *an ordinary chat*, but it also helps us to *move ahead, cheer up*, so that it isn't all about *downturns*.

(SG1, research interview)

Jette constructs a positive narrative about the support group, stating that it is not *an ordinary chat* but it is forum where they can *help each other to move on, cheer up*. Her wording is very positive and contrasts with the word *downturns*. The support group appears not only as a platform where serious issues can be discussed but also as a factor that facilitates constructive movement ahead and thereby the construction of agency.

Encounters with others

The third dominant theme in the respondents' narratives is concerned with ambivalence regarding their positioning as brain injured compared to the healthy population. Although to a different degree, the narratives indicate that each respondent constructs an identity as a person with ABI. For instance, during the discussion regarding availability of psychological services, the following exchange takes place:

KIRSTEN: What a task to live together with *us*.
JETTE: Yes, it is *horrible*.
LONE: Well, I/
PETER: Yeah, I do damn understand that *they* just leave.
(SG1, research interview)

Apparently, Kirsten positions herself as a burden toward her cohabitant, and her use of *us* indicates that she not only positions herself but the whole group as a burden. Furthermore, the use of the pronoun *us* can point at her narrative being influenced by the "us vs. them" discourse. Jette accepts this discourse and emphasizes it by saying it is *horrible*. Also, Peter confirms this discourse and his use of *they* witnesses again that he accepts the "us vs. them" discourse. This discourse can, on the one hand, strengthen the respondents' perception of being markedly different and so result in a greater passivity toward the surrounding world. On the other hand, it is also possible that the respondents actively choose these narratives to emphasize how difficult it is to live with ABI.

LONE: My husband's daughter is brain injured and he has stayed with me, that was surely not the case had he not been *well-trained in brain injury*.
(SG1, research interview)

It is noteworthy that Lone describes that her husband became *well-trained in brain injury*, whereby she indicates that the relatives need to be *well-trained* in order to tackle the challenges introduced by the brain injury. This may mean that she constructs an identity as a person that requires a special approach and specialized knowledge and thereby positions herself as markedly different from people without ABI. Others in the group also construct this identity.

INTERVIEWER: Are there any obvious changes (...) from before the brain injury and the way you are now?
(SG1, research interview)

This question provokes a longer discussion and, while Lone is describing her challenges, Kirsten suddenly interrupts and asks:

KIRSTEN: Now I've got to ask you [the interviewer] something, do you actually know anything about brain injury or is it in relation to something particular, or what?

INTERVIEWER: Well, I have worked as a personal assistant for a person with a disability, that is persons with cerebral palsy and that kind of thing.

(…)

KIRSTEN: Because, it was just to, you know, if you *could understand what we say.*

(…)

KIRSTEN: *If we talk about Russia and you think it's China.*

(…)

INTERVIEWER: Yes. We can understand you well.

KIRSTEN: No, no, it's just a curiosity … because then there were perhaps things that should be explained differently, if there is someone who doesn't know anything about it.

(SG1, research interview)

The discussion is interesting as it shows that Kirsten is positioning herself as different from the authors. Kirsten asks if the authors can *understand what we say*, which indicates that she constructs a small-d discourse where people with ABI develop their own language. She makes it even clearer with the metaphor *we talk about Russia and you think it's China* where her description also relates to different languages spoken in the respective countries. Her narrative further indicates that she, like Lone, constructs an identity as a person for whom a specialized knowledge is needed in order that she can be understood. This can also be influenced by a medical Capital-D discourse, where experts have the necessary knowledge in order to tackle persons with ABI. It is likely that she initially creates a positioning of the authors as ignorant. The interviewer rejects this position by saying *We can understand you well*, to which Kirsten replies *No, no, it's just a curiosity*, to signal a change as she realizes that she had positioned the authors as ignorant. Further reactions in response to the question "What do the respondents get out of the participation in the support group?" follow:

PETER: Understanding.

KIRSTEN: Just to figure out that *we* are not alone, that *we are not abnormal. We are not brain dead, we are just brain injured.*

PETER: Yes, yes, that's exactly right.

JETTE: That one is not the only one that is coping with it, there are also others in a similar situation like oneself, or the side-effects of the brain injury.

(SG1, research interview)

These narratives point to the fact that the respondents can mirror each other in the group. The fact that Kirsten uses the pronoun *we* illustrates that she constructs an identity of being like other persons with ABI and positions the others within the same level. Peter and Jette accept Kirsten's positioning of them being like other brain injury survivors. However, they also experience ambivalence that is reflected in the fact that they, on the one hand, construct an identity as brain injured, and on the other hand, do not wish to be perceived as abnormal. This ambivalence possibly challenges their identity reconstruction. The participation in the support group may reduce this ambivalence as the person can feel similarity with other people and thereby can perceive himself/herself as normal – which is underscored by Kirsten saying *we are not abnormal.* Furthermore, Kirsten expresses *We are not brain dead, we are just brain injured* where her use of *just* may indicate that she is attempting to normalize their condition. It can be expected that people with ABI feel insufficient on many fronts (e.g. as parents), but the support group becomes a haven where their diversity is welcome.

Peter's narratives witness that he several times takes the positioning of being different that the other group participants, to a degree inferior to the others.

PETER: And it is also *nice to see that there are others who are doing even worse than oneself ... no* (unclear?).

LONE: Yes, it is *sometimes nice that there is Peter to look at* and then one can think, wow I've really come far.

(SG1, research interview)

Peter expresses that it is *nice to see that there are others who are doing even worse than oneself* but right after he says *no*, which may mean that he has realized that others may find his narrative offensive. Lone subsequently uses a sentence constructed in a similar way as Peter's when she says that it is *sometimes nice that there is Peter to look at.* This is likely to mean that she does not accept Peter's narrative as she turns it against him, positioning Peter as less capable and to an extent inferior to her. Peter does not react to this and it is possible that his positioning as different in the group may make him less capable. It needs to be pointed out that the situation is surrounded by humor, and it is the authors' impression that humor and irony represent a way of talking about sensitive topics in the support group. Peter's positioning as inferior is however present several times, for instance when the respondents talk about the challenges after their injury:

PETER: It's because one has brain chaos … I mean thought chaos, sorry …
KIRSTEN: (…) *he is so sweet* …

(SG1, research interview)

Kirsten's response to Peter resembles a response that one would give to a child. It is likely that the group has adopted a position that Peter is indeed inferior, which is why he is positioned as more passive. This can be problematic as the support group is supposed to be a place where every participant is understood and recognized. Despite these differences, there are indications in the narratives that the respondents are positioning themselves as more equal among each other compared to the rest of the population. In connection with this, the respondents also describe that it is easier to meet other people with brain injuries than professionals and experts:

KIRSTEN: But it is just easier when it isn't an *occupational therapist* who
    sits there and tells you something, but that it is … *yeah, isn't it true*?
PETER: Yeah.
LONE: *We have tried it on our own skin*, haven't we?

(SG1, research interview)

These narratives show that Kirsten describes a discourse where *occupational therapists* and other professionals are not capable of understanding the challenges of life with ABI. In asking *yeah, isn't it true* she makes this discourse available to the other respondents. Both Peter and Lone accept it and Lone confirms it by saying *We have tried it on our own skin* whereby she strengthens this discourse in the group. They position themselves as different compared to others and it is possible that this discourse becomes part of the identity construction of the individual respondents. Interestingly, the group agrees that others cannot understand them, but at the same time they express dissatisfaction with being denoted "the brain injured" by others.

INTERVIEWER: (…) does it [the support group] provoke something else
    in you, or in relation to how you see yourself (…)?

(…)

LONE: It is also because it is more *legitimate* for us to say, you are also fuckin brain damaged (...) and that's what we can do here, can't we, that is, well you are brain dead, if there is someone else that comes and says that ... like that to me, then *I become terribly hurt and sorry*, but *if Peter says that then I just laugh* and tell him you are brain dead yourself.

(SG1, research interview)

This citation illustrates the ambivalence individuals with ABI experience when meeting other, non-injured people. In the support group it becomes more *legitimate* to make fun of their condition, but this is difficult to do outside the group. As Lone says, then *I become terribly hurt and sorry*. By adding that *if Peter says that then I just laugh* she positions Peter as equal to herself, which is in contrast to her previous positioning of Peter as inferior to her. Despite the fact that the respondents construct the identity as brain injured, it is only other brain injured individuals that are welcome to confirm this identity. The support group thereby gets a legitimating role, where the narratives confirmed by the group become available for the identity (re)construction of the individual respondents.

SG2

The group interaction has a good flow, but there is an imbalance in how much the three respondents speak, Patrick, in particular, frequently takes the lead. It is the author's impression that Patrick is relatively dominant in the group and will usually take control. The situation during the interview may therefore be similar to the situation during their regular meetings. The narratives and discourses that appear during the interview can therefore contribute to the understanding of the role this support group plays in the identity (re)construction of its participants. The central themes that appear in this interview are: (1) understanding of identity, (2) valuable identities, and (3) encounters with others.

Understanding of identity

During the interview the respondents discuss different labels, such as brain injured, disabled, and weird.

INTERVIEWER: Is there a difference in how you see yourselves when you are together in the [support] group and when you are together with other people?

(SG2, research interview)

Daniel describes a jogging event where some of the other participants were annoyed by him as he was constantly crossing their path.

DANIEL: (…) and my aunt had to go in and say that he was *brain
injured*, or *disabled*, she said.
JONAS: *It doesn't make any difference, anyway.*
PATRICK: *It is nicer.*
INTERVIEWER: Is it nicer?
JONAS: No, I'd rather be brain injured than disabled.
PATRICK: It is more confusing. There are many ways to be disabled.
Disabled, that can also be mentally ill.
DANIEL: *I'd rather be called brain injured.*
JONAS: Yes, the same for me.

(…) [Short interaction between the interviewer and Jonas, as the
interviewer has hard time understanding what Jonas says]

PATRICK: I don't want to be called either or, huhhuhhuh [everybody]. *I
want to be called weird.*
JONAS: That's what you are, weird.
PATRICK: *I am one of a kind*, and that's the way I've grown up.

(SG2, research interview)

Daniel describes that his Aunt has called him *brain injured* or *disabled.* The difference in the terms is not validated by Jonas who states
It doesn't make any difference, anyway. Patrick reacts by saying that
disabled, *it is nicer* and adds that disability is a broader term that refers
to a number of conditions by saying, *Disabled, that can also be mentally ill.* Patrick's narrative may mean that he understands himself as
disabled. By doing so, he may be positioning himself as different from
other persons with ABI (ID 2: sameness vs. difference). On the other
hand, it can also mean that he understands the term disability as a
meta category and thereby he is one of many. Daniel disagrees and
expresses *I'd rather be called brain injured*, which is validated by Jonas
who, apparently, has also constructed an identity as brain injured. The
interaction shows that Patrick offers a discourse regarding the term
disability, which is rejected by Daniel and Jonas who prefer to keep
their identity as brain injured. Subsequently, Patrick states that he is
dissatisfied with either term by saying *I want to be called weird.* Hereby,
he again distinguishes himself from others with ABI. It may be the
reason why he identifies himself to a great extent with the term

disabled. Using the term *weird* gives a possibility of distancing himself from any illness and approaching normality, as everybody can be weird. His subsequent response further emphasizes the point when he states *I am one of a kind*, which is a positive way to look at oneself. This may mean that Patrick indeed maintains his positioning as different from others with ABI, while he (re)constructs his identity from being disabled to being one of a kind. This interaction witnesses that there are different discourses that arise within the support group, and that the discourses can either be taken up and utilized in identity (re) construction of the respondents or rejected.

During the interview, the respondents describe several times the prejudices and biases they meet in their surroundings. This is likely to influence their identity (re)construction. Patrick continues his description regarding being weird.

INTERVIEWER: Yes, can you elaborate on that?
PATRICK: Well, it's because, to be weird and to be brain damaged, there are so many prejudices. *There are so many prejudices* when you say you are brain damaged, then people think ... when you for instance create a dating profile and you write that you have a brain injury, then people think right away that you are a *"spasso"* or they think you are *retarded*.
JONAS: That's what *they* really do.
INTERVIEWER: You also experience it, or?
JONAS: No, I haven't tried that. I have only had a profile twice, *I don't give a damn about it.* I'd much rather meet people face-to-face (unclear?), that other thing I don't bother.

(SG2, research interview)

In the interaction Patrick states that *There are so many prejudices* around brain injury. He constructs a discourse about others thinking that a brain injury equals spasticity or mental retardation. This can be linked to the Capital-D discourse that brain injury often results in intellectual disability. This is likely to be due to people making the connection between the brain and intelligence, and once the brain is injured, the intelligence must be reduced. Patrick's narrative illustrates that he meets this discourse in his private dating life, but he tries to distance himself from it by saying he is weird. Jonas validates this discourse and his use of *they* may mean that he is influenced by the "us vs. them" discourse. Hereby he positions himself as being "different" from the women he meets via online dating. Yet, his statements are somewhat contradictory – on the one hand, he says that he did not meet this prejudice, and on the other hand, he expresses a strong attitude against online dating *I don't give a damn about it*. The interaction between the respondents can indicate that Jonas validates Patrick's discourse and shows agency in that he has found other ways of dating. Jonas's narrative could also be influenced by the fact that the interviewer and observer were two younger females who do not have ABI.

The narratives of the respondents also show that they sometimes position themselves as equal to the normal population.

INTERVIEWER: (…) how do you look at yourselves when you are together with family or meet others on the street?

(…)

JONAS: Yeah, at that time [at the time of injury] I was just *completely brain damaged*, I couldn't figure out a shit. Neither *stand, walk or talk*, or other things. Today I *couldn't care less*, I play soccer and matches, and that type of thing and play (unclear?) together with *normal people* too. I can be together with both the brain injured and with normal folks, *so to speak*, right. And at my workplace, there are also only normal folks there, right?

(SG2, research interview)

Interestingly, Jonas positions himself as *completely brain damaged* right after his accident as he could not *stand, walk or talk*. This indicates that Jonas originally had a hard time to show agency due to the severity of his injury. However, he describes that today he *couldn't care less* and he plays soccer and participates in other activities with *normal people*, which illustrates an obvious change. It is possible that being together with other uninjured people is important to him since it gives him an opportunity to position himself as being equal to them. This can enhance his agency. Furthermore, his *so to speak* is likely to mean that he thinks that nobody is normal, whereby he strengthens his positioning as equal with both uninjured and injured. Patrick discusses the term normality.

PATRICK: But brain injury is a lot of things, (…), at some point we figured/ *we agreed that the word normal doesn't exist*. There is nothing that is called to be normal. Because *it is abnormal to be normal*, then the word doesn't exist.

JONAS: *Can I please say something*, yes, when I was at a Folk High School, and the first time I came there, *I stood up and said to everybody that I was brain damaged* and had problems remembering things they said or showed to me. I just said that to them. And *it was the coolest stay* I had there (…).

(SG2, research interview)

In the excerpt, Patrick continues his narrative and says *we agreed that the word normal doesn't exist.* Patrick's use of the word *we* indicate that there is a discourse in the support group that the term normal does not exist and that discourse is available for the identity (re)construction of all participants. This discourse may have positive consequences for the way the individuals understand themselves as it reduces the distance between normal and abnormal, as *it is abnormal to be normal.* Jonas joined at some point an ordinary Folk High School where he probably was the only pupil with ABI. He says *I stood up and said to everybody that I was brain damaged*, which indicates that his primary identity is to be a person with ABI and not, for instance, a pupil of the school. This is the point at which Jonas needs to articulate that he is different than other pupils. Later he states *it was the coolest stay*, which may mean that he did not necessarily experience the same prejudices and biases that Patrick previously described. It is possible that Jonas was approached in a similar way as other pupils after he had shared the fact about his condition. That points at Jonas not approving Patrick's narrative that normality does not exist. Notably, Jonas raises his finger (observation) and asks *Can I please say something*, which may mean that he is finding it difficult to have his say, and is still actively constructing his identities during the interview. The authors' general impressions are that it is challenging for Jonas to construct longer and coherent narratives on several occasions, which is why he sticks to merely confirming others' narratives (observation). It is possible that Jonas's linguistic impairment becomes a barrier regarding his manifestation of agency. The support group can thereby exert a negative influence on Jonas as it increases his passivity. The interviewer experiences several times that Jonas's language is difficult to understand. This can also be the case when he is with other people, which is why he often articulates short and blunt sentences. This is possibly also emphasized by him smiling a lot and praising the others. It is likely that the other people in the group, including the authors, position Jonas as very positive in one way, but also as more passive regarding his utilization of discourses to construct his own understanding of the world.

Identity as different is also discussed earlier in the interview:

INTERVIEWER: What do you get out of this [participation in support group]?

(…)

PATRICK: But the same way is *we call the pedagogues for "spasserpasser"* [Danish derogatory term for helpers of persons with disabilities] and that kind of thing. We make fun of things, 'cause one can't cry over it all the time. One can as well take it as a joke, that is to make fun of it.

JONAS: Yes, take it with humor.

DANIEL: *We wouldn't be able to do anything else, if we couldn't make fun of it.*

(SG2, research interview)

Patrick describes here that *we call the pedagogues for "spasserpasser."* This wording indicates that his positioning may nevertheless be closer to people with brain injuries, as the term "spasser" in Danish (meaning "spaz" in English) is a slang word for spastic cerebral palsy. The use of the pronoun *we* indicates that the group and perhaps many people with ABI use that term for their pedagogues. Both Jonas and Daniel validate Patrick's small d-discourse regarding making fun of their condition. Daniel's narrative indicates that he takes over the discourse when he says *We wouldn't be able to do anything else, if we couldn't make fun of it.* This may mean that Daniel to an extent sees Patrick as his role model, and would like to resemble him. Alternatively, it may mean that Daniel merely validates Patrick's narrative and their interaction means that, together, they construct an identity as people that can make fun of their condition.

Valuable identities

Another dominant theme in the interview is the construction of valuable identities.

INTERVIEWER: (…) is there a reason that it became this very support group?

(…)

PATRICK: And one way or another, now I will again appear as the
"captain," as the *"captain"* that has everything under control, but
one way or another I do see the support group as a *little child*, in
many ways, don't get me wrong, but tell me, *can they manage
without me?* (...)
JONAS: It's so *cool* that you do it, Patrick.

(SG2, research interview)

Patrick describes the support group as his *little child*, which indicates
that he positions himself as a caring parent who takes responsibility for
the other group participants, whereby he constructs a valuable identity.
He uses the word *"captain"* more than once, which points to him being
aware that he is taking this position. This is further emphasized by him
asking *can they manage without me?* The support group has thereby
become a forum where Patrick feels he can contribute, something that can
be important for his identity (re)construction. It is also possible that
Patrick's narrative is influenced by postmodernist societal discourse,
where he actively contributes to society. Jonas expresses that it is *cool*,
which may mean that he validates Patrick's identity as being valuable for
their group. Moreover, his reaction suggests that, to an extent, he might
wish to be like Patrick, i.e. someone who is able to make a difference for
the group. Patrick's positioning as the *"captain"* of the group may include
a father-like identity, where the other group participants are to be taken
care of. This becomes clear from the interaction below:

PATRICK: I was *quite impressed* with Daniel who last Thursday on his
own took care of the shopping for the meeting in the group.
Because, I was thinking now I've got to prepare that shopping list
and everything and then he wrote that well, he could take care of
it. And that was *quite positive*.
JONAS: Yes, *he did it*.
PATRICK: Yes, actually *he did it* (unclear?), that was cool ....
DANIEL: I managed to do a to-do list because he [another participant
of the group] went *totally to pieces* last.

(SG2, research interview)

In the interaction, Patrick describes that he was *quite impressed* with
Daniel and that was *quite positive*. This choice of words can be related
to the way a parent talks to his/her child and thereby illustrates the
parent-like identity that Patrick constructs while he positions Daniel as
minor. Subsequently, Jonas and Patrick together praise Daniel by stating *he did it*. Daniel first accepts this positioning and starts a

description how he took care of the task since the other participant was about to go *totally to pieces*. This interaction confirms that it is legitimate to talk about positive qualities of the individual participants in the group and confirm each other in it. However, the following interaction also shows that Daniel attempts to distance himself from being positioned as minor.

DANIEL: And I don't know/ Patrick he *has a hard time to cope with such things*, so ...
PATRICK: Yeah, well, *I could have done it*, but I'd rather be *free*.
DANIEL: Yeah, sure you can, but as you say, you'd rather be free.

(SG2, research interview)

Now Daniel constructs a positioning of Patrick as a person who *has a hard time to cope with such things*, which is rejected by Patrick who says *I could have done it*. Interestingly, Daniel in this case positions himself as being responsible and caring toward Patrick. It is possible that Daniel is trying to get out of Patrick's positioning of him as a person who needs to be taken care of. Patrick does not accept this counter-positioning and expresses that he could have taken care of the task but preferred to be *free*, which is accepted by Daniel. Apparently, counter-positioning sometimes emerges in the group. Patrick is however able to maintain his position, which Daniel approves, and thereby he remains more passive. The fact that Daniel adopts Patrick's discourses may again mean that Daniel sees Patrick as a role model. It needs to be remembered that Patrick is 11 years older, which may contribute to the fact that Daniel is not able to maintain his positioning. There is a tendency during the interview that Patrick positions himself as better-off than the other respondents.

PATRICK: And I am one of the old dogs ... I think I am the only one of the very *old boys* together with [mentions a name of another person].

(SG2, research interview)

The narrative indicates that Patrick positions himself as more valuable compared to the other respondents in the group due to him being one of the *old boys*. This indicates that his narrative is influenced by the small-d discourse where experience is paired with status. Notably, however, on several occasions both Daniel and Jonas point out the linguistic mistakes in Patrick's language. For instance, Patrick describes that he uses his cell phone to remember appointments and states that without it, he would be "last."

DANIEL: Are you *"last"*?
PATRICK: *"Last,"* one is completely at the mercy of/
DANIEL: *Not "last," but lost.*
PATRICK: Yeah, lost, lost, you *nitpicker*.

(SG2, research interview)

The interaction shows that Patrick is initially not aware of his wrong pronunciation of the word "lost" and does not respond to Daniel's comment. Only when Daniel becomes very clear about his correction by saying *Not "last," but lost*, Patrick modifies his pronunciation. Strikingly, Patrick calls Daniel a *nitpicker*, whereby he expresses his irritation with Daniel's correction of his language. This illustrates that Daniel positions Patrick as a person with linguistic difficulties and thereby does not validate Patrick's positioning as being better-off. This is interesting as Daniel could have refrained from correcting Patrick. It is possible that Daniel dislikes the fact that Patrick often takes control and appears to be the best-functioning member of the group, which is why he tries to get him down to his level. Nevertheless, the interaction is carried out in a friendly tone. The authors gain the impression that there is a good comradeship and solidarity in the support group. The respondents also meet privately and engage themselves in the Danish Association of Brain Injured, which is especially the case for Patrick.

Encounter with others

During the interview several positionings regarding the encounter with others with and without ABI emerge. The analysis presents them in this order.

Not only Patrick positions himself as different from other people with ABI, we also see this in Jonas.

INTERVIEWER: (...) What does it give you [participation in the support group]? If we start with you, Jonas.
JONAS: It *gives me incredibly much joy*, I'd say because (unclear?) the positive the people are in this group here because *many of my other friends are simply depressed* or sad or angry at everything, everything and everybody, right? And that I can't use for anything.
INTERVIEWER: Is it somebody from those who come in the support group that are like that, or what do you say?
JONAS: No, it is at that coffee bar, where we are.
INTERVIEWER: Ok, I see.

JONAS: Where I also come every day. And they have *always* problems with their pedagogues or supervisors or something and I don't feel like listening to that and I say it to them. I can't use that for anything.

INTERVIEWER: Is it then that you experience something different in this support group?

JONAS: It is in the way that they *have all these problems* in their heads and that's not my case.

INTERVIEWER: Is it because you come to the support group that you don't have that, or?

JONAS: It's because I think of my life in *a positive way*, and they don't, they see always only *the negative things*, right?

PATRICK: But our group is generally speaking very *positive*.

(SG2, research interview)

Jonas describes that the support group *gives me incredibly much joy*, which is due to the fact that *many of my other friends are simply depressed* and *always* have problems. His narrative expresses that he values the positive atmosphere that governs this support group, which is different from what he experiences when meeting others with ABI. Notably he uses the word *joy* when talking about the support group and the word *depressed* about his other friends. Likewise, he states that he thinks of his life *a positive way*, in contrast to the others who only see *the negative things*. This illustrates that Jonas constructs his identity along positive values, which are present in the support group. His use of antonyms underscores that he positions himself as different from others with ABI. He also states *they have all these problems*, which is not his case. His use of pronouns *they* and *I* indicate that his narrative is influenced by the "us vs. them" discourse. The narratives that emerge suggest that this support group is based on positive values. This is likely to influence the narratives of the group's participants. On the other hand, there is a risk that worries and negative feelings are not validated in the support group, which is something that could be problematic, as such feelings are quite natural after ABI. However, Jonas does not attribute the positive attitude to the support group, but rather to himself and his personality. In general, the support group is referred to in a positive way and the respondents appear to be very engaged.

Regarding encounters with others without ABI, during interview it is Patrick in particular who positions himself as different.

INTERVIEWER: Is there a *difference* in the way you see yourself when you are among others, or in the support group and others?

(...)

PATRICK: When I am together with the support group, I am *more foolish* than when I am, so to speak, together with *traditional people*. I am more *serious*, and more, I must say I have to take care what I say and/

JONAS: I don't give a damn.

PATRICK: I could get the idea to have something to drink together with the support group (unclear?) or when I am alone but I would *never dream of* drinking anything with my family or together with strangers, so to speak.

(SG2, research interview)

Patrick describes here that he is *more foolish* when he is together with his support group compared to *traditional people*, where he is more *serious*, whereby he positions himself as clearly different from others without ABI. It is also interesting that he uses the term *traditional people*, which may be linked to the fact that he previously described that the word normal does not exist. Therefore, he seems to have found a new synonym for healthy/normal people. The contrast to *traditional people* is markedly emphasized by his choice of saying *never dream of* when he talks about drinking alcohol together with others without ABI. It should also be noticed that the interviewer asks if there is a *difference*, which implicitly suggests a positioning of respondents as different from others without ABI. Patrick accepts this positioning, which is not the case for Jonas.

JONAS: Well, my family really take the piss out of me. They just *accept* me completely, right from day one.

INTERVIEWER: So, do you feel *different* when you are together with your family?

JONAS: Nope, *not at all.*

INTERVIEWER: How's about when you are together with people you don't know that well?

JONAS: I don't care, if they don't like me, they don't have to talk to me, this is just the way it is. I can't use it for anything, I damn can't. If they want to see me wrong, then look. I don't *give a damn.* I can't use it for anything.

(SG2, research interview)

Jonas describes that his family *accepts* him and can joke about his condition, which illustrates that he does not feel any different in their company. He also expresses that he does not *give a damn* regarding what other people think of his condition. This points at high agency since he does not depend on others' opinions. It is also evident that Jonas distances himself from the positioning that the interviewer suggests – being *different* than his family, which he rejects by saying *not at all*. However, it is also possible that his rough attitude and description reflects that he may have had unpleasant experiences with others and, as a result, he rejects the negative comments of others. Furthermore, Jonas's narrative appears somewhat blunt. Daniel also answers the same question from the interviewer:

DANIEL: No, I don't think there is a difference, well yeah, if I come to people that I see for the first time, then yes, and my family knows all about it. Then I become *very silent* and observant (…).

(SG2, research interview)

Daniel describes that he does not experience himself as different when being together with his family, whereby he does not accept the positioning offered by the interviewer. Subsequently he corrects himself and describes that he is *very silent* when encountering new people and indicates that he is reserved before he becomes familiar with other people. This can have played a role also in the current interview where Daniel originally appears more silent and tired (observation).

The above described interactions illustrate that the three respondents tackle encounters with other people without ABI differently. A possible explanation may lie in the visibility of their impairments, where both Patrick and Daniel, contrary to Jonas, do not have any visible impairments.

PATRICK: But, but on the other hand, I had a female friend who got new colleagues at work and then there was one, then one of the new colleagues came to her and said: "I've been told you are brain damaged, well I don't see anything" and the girl [gives her name], it was her, became quite angry. "Yes, it may be that you don't see how I am. It may be that I *look very normal* and speak normally, but you can't see *how I feel inside my head*" (…).

(SG2, research interview)

Patrick describes how his friend experienced the fact that others could not see that she had a brain injury. His friend rejected the comment of a work colleague saying that, although she *looked very normal*, others do not have access into *how I feel inside my head* and so they cannot evaluate her condition. It is interesting that Patrick chooses to bring this example into the interview, as it is not his own experience.

Possibly, he feels a great sympathy for his friend. And he may also relate to the example and position both himself and his friend as victims facing the invisible challenges after ABI. This furthermore indicates that there is a discourse in the group regarding the fact that others without ABI cannot relate to them and understand what it is like to have a brain injury, not the least because many consequences are not obvious. Patrick continues:

PATRICK: (…) It is also it is this thing that is hard with brain injury sometimes, that on the surface, we appear *normal* and *well-functioning*, many of us. It is ten times easier to understand a person that sits in a wheelchair or can't use the right arm than a person who is brain injured and who is on the surface articulated and has motor skills.

INTERVIEWER: Is it also what you experience, Daniel? That that can/

DANIEL: Yes, I have often experienced this where, well, you don't look like someone who is brain damaged. You don't look disabled at all.

JONAS: There, I have been a little *more lucky*, one could say. You can see it on me.

DANIEL: Yes, on [gives a name of another participant of the group] one can also hear it, but *that is not the case for me or Patrick.*

JONAS: No, that's right, you both speak well.

(SG2, research interview)

In these narratives, Patrick describes that many people with brain injuries can appear *normal* and *well-functioning*, which is validated by Daniel. Contrary to what they described earlier in the analysis about not feeling any different than other non-brain injured persons, this narrative indicates that it is not that easy after all, due to their invisible impairments. Jonas positions himself as "*more lucky*" due to his visible impairments. In general, however, it is more challenging to have invisible impairments as well as visible physical impairment(s). Daniel confirms Jonas's positioning, and states that one can hear in another's language if they are injured or not, but *that is not the case for me or Patrick.* By doing so, Daniel positions him and Patrick even further away from Jonas due to his obvious linguistic problems. It needs to be remembered, however, that Patrick also makes linguistic mistakes.

As mentioned earlier, there is a strong feeling of solidarity in the support group.

INTERVIEWER: Have you experienced any changes regarding yourselves from before you'd joined this support group and to now?

(…)

DANIEL: Yes, back in time, I had quite many … *non-brain injured* friends and it was so, well, they didn't say it loud, but I could clearly feel it, oh no, here comes the guy, him, *the brain damaged* and *disabled*, now I'd must take care and make sure we are not too much. On the contrary, when I now ring Patrick or one of the others, well, we *are just on the same level*.

PATRICK: (…) take more people as they are and then join the support group where we've agreed [gives names of the participants] we've agreed that the support group *has served its purpose*. Because the purpose was to create a network. And I and we have actually agreed that we have got some really *good friends* in the support group.

(SG2, research interview)

Daniel's narrative indicates that he previously felt misunderstood by his *non-brain injured* friends, who positioned him as *the brain damaged* and *disabled* one. The contrast in his word choice *non-brain injured* vs. *the brain damaged* indicates that Daniel, at some time earlier, constructed his identity as brain injured, thereby positioning himself as clearly different from other healthy individuals (ID 2: sameness vs. difference). He describes that now he can just phone Patrick and they *are just on the same level.* His use of the pronoun *we* and words like *same level* further indicate that he positions himself at an equal level with other individuals with ABI and describes a discourse that all ABI survivors are the same. However, this is in contrast to his previous narrative where he positioned himself as being different from Jonas. It is nevertheless likely that Daniel positions himself as being more equal to Jonas than to other non-brain injured persons. Subsequently, Patrick describes that they have become *good friends* and that the support group *has served its purpose.* The fact that Patrick chooses to include the purpose of the support group in his narrative is interesting. This may reflect that he sees himself as being responsible for the group and therefore would like to emphasize the positive change the group has brought about. Moreover, it indicates that he constructs his identity along the values of the support group.

Discussion

The interaction in SG1 indicates that, when being together in the support group, it is legitimate to construct narratives that position the participants as insufficient, dependent, and different from others. On several occasions the respondents confirm each other's narratives in this sense and thereby create common ground in the group. The common ground discourse of being insufficient, dependent, and different may play an inhibitory role with respect to the identity (re)construction of the individual respondents as the respondents become less influential over their surroundings. On the other hand, the analysis also shows that the respondents are capable of freeing themselves from these discourses whereby they sometimes obtain an opportunity to look beyond their own limitations. This points at increased agency and can have a positive impact on identity (re)construction. These results are in line with the study of Lexell et al. (2013). Finally, the understanding and acceptance they meet in the support group can positively influence the tension regarding several identity dilemmas suggested by the narrative identity theory of Bamberg , De Fina, and Schiffrin (2011). These dilemmas are concerned with feeling a constant versus a changed self over time, feeling the same as or different from others, and experiencing oneself as an active agent regarding one's own identity versus remaining passive (Bamberg, 2011; Bamberg, 2014; Bamberg et al., 2011). This in turn can strengthen the individual's self-perception and self-confidence. The group can thus contribute with psychological resources (Jones et al., 2012).

The interactions in SG2 show that it is legitimate in the support group to position oneself as brain injured and thereby different from others. However, at the same time the respondents experience ambiguity regarding their navigation in the identity dilemma regarding same versus different from others. One respondent (Patrick) opposes this by constructing an identity as weird. The interaction demonstrates that the respondents, on several occasions, confirm each other in their positioning, whereby they create common discourses in the support group. The analysis also showed that there is a discourse regarding the term "normality" in the group, with a fluid transition between normal and abnormal. It is possible that this can be beneficial for the participants' identity (re)construction. Additionally, it is apparent that all respondents have a strong affiliation to the support group where they have redefined their own values according to the positive values and ideals that the support group is based on. In particular, Patrick constructs a strong disability identity in alignment with his engagement in the support group, which is likely to positively influence his identity (re)construction.

The study was aimed at answering the following question: In which way does the support group influence the identity (re)construction of the brain injured individual and what is the effect of self-narratives in this process? Respondents in SG1 are especially challenged by the loss of the life – and thereby of the self – they once had. Also, the study by Nochi (1997) points at the fact that survivors of traumatic brain injury can experience a void and emptiness between their former and current self. The void illustrates the period after injury where they do not have a recollection of memories due to the injury. In contrast, the respondents in SG2 seem to have accepted the injury as separate to themselves. This is likely to reflect the time that passed since their injury (see Table 11.1). It is likely that, with time, the brain injury is embedded in the self as indicated for example, by the use of personal pronouns like *I* when describing the present situation and him when referring to the past (Body, Muskett, Perkins, & Parker, 2013). It appears that the respondents in both support groups feel a need to become recognized as changed. But this does not necessarily mean that their former self has been completely lost due to the injury. As Gelech and Desjardins (2011) point out, the individual with a brain injury preserves the inner self and the restoration process is influenced by processes of delegitimization, invalidation, negotiation, and resistance, which have a critical impact on the post-injury (re)construction of the self. The respondents in SG1 appear to be subject to this discourse regarding the discontinued self. Meeting the discourse in their non-injured surroundings can negatively influence their navigation regarding the identity dilemma of constant vs. changed self (Bamberg et al., 2011). The others in the group expect the discontinuation, while an individual with ABI experiences themselves as continuous over time. The support groups can help in this process, as the members of the group typically do not have any prior knowledge of the injured person and thereby meet them as they currently are. By doing so, the injured individual gets an opportunity to integrate their former self into the current one. On the other hand, it can be argued that if the discourse of being changed and different after injury is dominating the support group, then the support group itself may hamper the integration process and thereby inhibit identity (re)construction. A different situation is seen in SG2. Here the long chronicity after injury onset has probably created a situation where the former self of the respondents was not lost, but more likely forgotten, both by the respondents themselves and by their relatives and friends.

The challenges connected to identity changes can be linked to an idealized view of the past (Cloute et al., 2008), which can also explain the differences seen between SG1 and SG2. In SG1, the ages of the respondents at injury onset are significantly higher than those of the respondents in SG2 (see Table 11.1). It is plausible that respondents in SG1 are more challenged as they have already established themselves in their lives before the injury and hence look at the past as the "good old times" (Iverson, Lange, Brooks, & Rennison, 2010). In contrast to this, the relatively low age at injury onset in SG2 may mean that each individual's identity process was only just evolving and, therefore, they do not experience this loss to the same degree. However, the potential impact of brain injury acquired at an early age must not be underestimated. The early onset may mean that the person experiences a lack of opportunity to develop themselves as they feel as if everything was taken away from them. Participation in a support group may in this case be helpful for identity (re)construction if the support group is capable of constructing valuable alternative identities that the group participants can use.

As evident from the analysis, the respondents are subject to the postmodern discourse present in society. This dictates how they ought to be and what they should achieve in life. According to Brinkmann (2014), life in Western societies is characterized by a pronounced acceleration demanding that each and every individual stays on track, is active, and performs well. This is especially dominant within education and work, where each individual is expected to evolve through lifelong learning and achieve self-realization . Participation in the labor market is therefore one of the most important sources for identity formation in society today. This understanding of oneself is also paralleled in people's social and private lives, where they are expected to strive for personal development in order to become the best possible "versions" of themselves (Brinkmann, 2014). In accordance with this, the respondents in this study also strive to get a job where they can develop, and to be good, energetic parents who partake in many of the children's activities. This discourse can, on the one hand, facilitate post-injury identity (re)construction by emphasizing the active attitude and participation required from the injured individual. On the other hand, the high demands can pressure the individual to strive toward the high ideal, which in turn can enhance feelings of insufficiency. This seems to be present in SG1. Here the respondents construct narratives where they position themselves as insufficient parents in the light of all the demands that a good parent must live up to. While this discourse enables them to maintain a feeling of being in the same position as all the other parents, it also hampers their identity (re)construction as a "good" parent identity is unachievable. Furthermore, this can be even more problematic as their parent identity appears to have become the dominant identity, particularly because other identities, such as their work identity, can no longer be maintained. Regarding SG2, it is possible that their more positive views on their lives is rooted in the fact that they are all employed. Although only in light duty jobs, their active work identity may explain why they do not feel as insufficient as respondents in SG1 and may facilitate the construction of positive narratives, which strengthens their identity (re)construction. In their study, Mozo-Dutton, Simpson, and Boot (2012) have described that the individual's self-perception is determined by the degree to which physical and cognitive impairment influence different activities. It is the perceived importance of the activity that determines whether the individual experiences identity loss or not. Although this study was performed with people suffering from multiple sclerosis, its conclusions are likely to apply to the brain injured population as well. Given that three out of four respondents in SG1 suffered brain injury during the life phase where parenting plays a prominent role, activities related to parenting are perceived as highly important. None of the respondents in SG1 are working and attachment to the labor market is therefore likely to be perceived as less important in SG1. A reversed pattern is seen in SG2, where none of the respondents have become parents yet, but they are all working. Working is thus subjectively perceived as important. They experience that, despite their impairments, they are able to contribute at work, which gives them a feeling of meaningfulness and creates a basis for positive self-narratives.

In general, the analysis demonstrates that the respondents experience themselves as seriously affected by the brain injury and that they therefore have to go through a hard adjustment process. It is plausible that they may feel the need to talk about difficult topics with the support group. Interestingly, there is a difference regarding how well the two support groups welcome and recognize the negative narratives and individual differences. In SG1, the respondents share many negative narratives (see e.g. *Lone: my daughter has moved out from home because of me …*) and the support group thereby becomes a platform where even difficult or taboo topics can be taken up. In contrast, SG2 has a positive tone governing their meetings (see e.g. *Jonas: It gives me incredibly much joy, I'd say, because (unclear?) the positive people are in this groups* and *Patrick: But our group is generally speaking very positive*). This difference may be due to the fact that SG1 was only formed recently and their respondents have lived with ABI for a much shorter period of time compared to SG2, who have been in touch for several years and their injuries happened many years ago (see Table 11.1). The shorter duration of living with a brain injury is likely to mean a lower level of ease with this new life-changing situation. Hence, the respondents in SG1 have a greater need to talk about the injury-related challenges. As Schwartzberg (1994) describes, being able to share the pain and sorrow in, for example, a support group is perceived as a helping factor toward the feeling of being accepted. This can facilitate identity (re)construction if the support group assists the individual to leave the negative narratives behind. Furthermore, to be able to support peers with ABI in a support group is also seen as valuable (Schwartzberg, 1994). The fact that the negative narratives are not welcome in SG2 could mean that an individual with such a need would not be recognized and hence potentially not helped with their transition toward more constructive narratives and agency. This, however, does not seem to be the case in SG2. The lack of emotional narratives in SG2 may also be rooted in the fact that the male respondents in SG2 did not wish to be positioned as vulnerable when facing the female interviewers and observers.

The support group can evidently facilitate the construction of valuable identities. Both SG1 and SG2 articulate new values and the analysis indicates that, together, they construct new and valuable identities. For instance, in SG1 both Peter and Kirsten describe that they are more in touch with their emotional side. This personal ability is apparently cherished in the support group where it is legitimate. Also, in SG2, all respondents describe their positive approach to life and contribution to the peer community, where Patrick in particular presents narratives regarding his (valuable) identity as someone who contributes to the running of the support group (*Patrick: And one way or another, now I will again appear as the "captain"*). Hence, it has positive consequences if the individual redefines their goals and values according to, for example, the values in the disability community or a patient organization. Thereby, it is evident that the support group benefits its participants in the presence of a chronic condition.

The analysis showed that the respondents in both support groups experienced ambivalence regarding their identity dilemmas about being same as vs. different from others. On the one hand, they position themselves as equal to people without brain injury, and, on the other, they construct the identity of a sick person – not least in the light of the demands from their peers, which they find difficult to deal with. This identity dilemma is approached in different ways within the two support groups. The respondents' narratives show that they meet a lack of understanding from the outside world, which is accentuated, in some cases, by the invisible nature of their problems. It is possible that it is this invisibility that contributes to this identity dilemma: physically, the respondents are similar to other non-injured persons, but they are also different as they cannot meet, for instance, the expectations regarding their social engagement and roles.

Informal support groups offer the possibility for identity renegotiation (Shadden & Agan, 2004). It is evident from the narratives that the identity dilemma "being same as vs. different from others" is influenced by the Capital D-discourse that presents persons with ABI as retarded (see Nochi, 1998). If this discourse is validated by the group, then it is made accessible for the identity (re)construction of the individual respondents. The support group can hereby maintain the individual in one position (e.g. as being different) or push toward the construction of a new/altered identity. Obviously, it can be problematic if a person constructs an identity as being incapable and misunderstood, and this identity is then validated and strengthened by the support group. In such a case, the individual is likely to maintain a more passive approach while the support group contributes to the stigmatization of the individual. Implicitly, this may lead to a rejection of the disability identity (Bogart, 2015). A strong connection to a group of disabled peers is associated with lower levels of depression and anxiety (Bogart, 2015). Additionally, individuals with ABI often develop strategies to cope with the negative labels, such as being retarded (Nochi, 1998). A clear example of such a strategy is presented by SG2, whose respondents discuss the notion of "normality" and a discourse of "*normality does not exist*" emerges. It appears that SG2 is capable, to a higher degree, of constructing useful discourses that can be used by the individual respondents in their identity (re)construction, when compared to SG1. Again, the longer duration of SG2 may at least partially be the explanation. However, the analysis clearly shows that both support groups contribute to a normalization of the condition of being brain injured (see e.g. *Kirsten: Wwe are not abnormal. We are not brain dead, we are just brain injured*). This indicates that the opportunity to reflect upon one's situation and discuss it with peers, who know how it feels, is of a special importance. Apparently, peer discussions are capable of reducing stigmatization and increasing the agency of the affected individuals. It can therefore be argued that peer support groups have a legitimizing function beyond what professional therapists can offer. For instance, as witnessed by the narratives in SG1, it is legitimate in the group to call each other brain damaged, however, if a stranger (a non-brain injured person) says this, it is taken as an offense. Thus, the peer support groups are, on the one hand, able to confirm the identity of being ill or different, and, on the other hand, they can offer discourses that bring the condition closer to normality.

The discourses that are based on "them vs. us" are also present in relation to the public sector. Denmark is a welfare state and social services are therefore free of charge. As mentioned in the introduction, upon completed hospitalization, all responsibility regarding retraining and rehabilitation is placed with the local municipalities. However, the public services dealing with patients in the post-acute and chronic stages of injury are often criticized. The criticism is rooted in a lack of neurological competencies, unwillingness to deal with demanding cases, exaggerated focus on administration, and meaningless documentation (as part of the new public management approach), leading to neglecting the person behind the injury and an ineffective application of resources (Berger & Bonfils, 2011; Olsen & Bonfils, 2013; Rasmussen, Navne, Fulgsang, & Kruse, 2014; Wiuff, Navne, & Olesen, 2010). The perceptions of individuals with ABI in the current analysis also point to persistent challenges and misunderstandings between the individuals with ABI and the public sector. The field of brain injury rehabilitation is still hampered by barriers, contractions, and conflicts that prevent the successful implementation of comprehensive bio–psycho–social models (Glintborg, Mateu, & Høgsbro, 2016). Nochi (1998) explains that the prejudices and views of the person are often in sharp contrast to the way the person understands themselves. It is likely that this discrepancy has a disturbing impact on the identity (re)construction process. The "us vs. them" discourse present (particularly in SG1) can lead to a more passive position, where the individual with ABI creates a discourse of being excluded from participation in their broader surroundings. Yet participation in a support group can counterbalance this effect and enhance social participation in general (McLean et al., 2012), thereby playing a preventive role against isolation and social withdrawal.

Limitations

Although the conversational data provided a more natural context compared to in-depth individual interviewing (Bevan & Bevan, 1999), they still represent the perspective of the individual respondents. Furthermore, the focus group interviews may not, due to their social setting, shed adequate light on individual views, resulting in an underreporting of more atypical outlooks and individual perspectives (Halkier, 2010). It is also possible that the significantly different social background between the interviewer and the respondents may have resulted in a bias (Karpatschof, 2007).

Conclusions

The results demonstrate that all respondents have experienced changes regarding their own identity after ABI. They further show that the support groups can provide discourses and positioning, which can be used in the individual identity (re)construction processes. In both support groups, the postmodernistic discourse regarding how things "should" be was present. This discourse puts high demands on each individual and requires that they deliver on all fronts and perform well in each aspect of life. This can be particularly difficult to achieve for individuals with ABI. As a consequence, a person with ABI tends to strive for something that is unachievable and ends up with an identity dominated by feelings of insufficiency and dependency. It seems possible to free oneself from these dominating discourses if within the support group. Both support groups have been able to redefine their values over time and construct valuable identities in alignment with the values that create the basis for the support groups, such as understanding and recognition. It is likely that this has positively influenced identity (re)construction, as it facilitates navigation between the different identity dilemmas. The analysis also revealed that the support groups are used to talking about the challenges the respondents meet when dealing with both the healthy/uninjured population and the public service system. Here the prevalent discourse is "us vs. them." The respondents experience ambivalence when being together with uninjured persons, as they meet misunderstanding and even opposition (e.g. being viewed as lazy). They position themselves as equal among peers in the support group, pointing to the fact that participation in the support group contributes to the normalization of their condition. Yet, they draw a distinction between those whose impairments are visible vs. those whose are invisible.

References

Bamberg, M. (2011). Who am I? Narration and its contribution to self and identity. *Theory & Psychology*, 21(1), 3–24.

Bamberg, M. (2014). Narrative practices versus capital-*D* discourses: Ways of investigating family. *Journal of Family Theory & Review*, 6(1), 132–136.

Bamberg, M., De Fina, A., & Schiffrin, D. (2011). Discourse and identity construction. In S. Schwartz, K. Luyckx, & V. Vignoles (Eds.), *Handbook of identity theory and research, Vols 1 and 2* (pp. 177–199). New York: Springer.

Bates, T. (2005). The expression of compassion in group psychotherapy. In P. Gilbert (Ed.), *Compassion: Conceptualisations, research and use in psychotherapy* (pp. 369–386). London: Routledge.

Bellon, M., Sando, S., Crocker, R., Farnden, J., & Duras, M. (2017). Information, connection and giving back: Peer support outcomes for families following acquired brain injury in South Australia. *Health & Social Care in the Community*, 25(1), 204–214.

Berger, N. P. & Bonfils, I. S. (2011). ØNSKES: Kommuner med høj faglighed. *AKF Nyt*, 2, 21–22.

Bevan, S. & Bevan, K. (1999). Interviews: Meaning in groups. In I. Parker & B. D. Network (Eds.), *Critical textwork. An introduction to varieties of discourse analysis* (pp. 15–28). Buckingham, UK: Open University Press.

Boden-Albala, B., Litwak, E., Elkind, M. S., Rundek, T., & Sacco, R. L. (2005). Social isolation and outcomes post stroke. *Neurology*, 64(11),1888–1892.

Body, R., Muskett, T., Perkins, M., & Parker, M. (2013). Your injury, my accident: Talking at cross-purposes in rehabilitation after traumatic brain injury. *Brain Injury*, 27(12), 1356–1363.

Bogart, K. R. (2015). Disability identity predicts lower anxiety and depression in multiple sclerosis. *Rehabilitation Psychology*, 60(1), 105–109.

Brinkmann, S. & Kvale, S. (2005). Confronting the ethics of qualitative research. *Journal of Constructivist Psychology*, 18(2), 157–181.

Brinkmann, S. (2014) *Stå fast - et opgør med tidens udviklingstrang* [Stand Firm: Resisting the Self-Improvement Craze]. Copenhagen, Denmark: Gyldendal Forlag.

Carey, M. A. (2011). Focusing on research credibility: Grounding focus groups in principles and ethics. *International Journal of Qualitative Methods*, 10(4), 536–537.

Cloute, K., Mitchell, A., & Yates, P. (2008). Traumatic brain injury and the construction of identity: A discursive approach. *Neuropsychological Rehabilitation*, 18(5–6), 651–670.

Finlayson, M. & Cho, C. C. (2011). A profile of support group use and need among middle-aged and older adults with multiple sclerosis. *Journal of Gerontological Social Work*, 54(5), 475–493.

Gelech, J. M. & Desjardins, M. (2011). I am many: The reconstruction of self following acquired brain injury. *Qualitative Health Research*, 21(1), 62–74.

Glintborg, C. (2015). Grib mennesket. En konceptuel og empirisk undersøgelse af koordineret rehabilitering: objektivt bio-psyko-social udbytte for voksne med erhvervet hjerneskade samt klienters og pårørendes oplevelse af rehabiliteringen med og uden kommunal coordination [Seize the self! An empirical mixed methods study of the bio–psyko–social recovery outcomes and perceptions of a coordinated neurorehabilitation program]. Ph.D. thesis, The Faculty of Humanities. Aalborg, Denmark: Aalborg Universitetsforlag. Available at: www.hcci.aau.dk/digitalAssets/129/129472_chalotte_glintborg_phd-afhandling.pdf.

Glintborg, C., Mateu, N. C., & Høgsbro, K. (2016). Contradictions and conflicts in brain injury rehabilitation. A systematic inquiry into models of rehabilitation. *Scandinavian Journal of Disability Research*, 18(4), 369–383.

Hagger, B. F. (2011). An exploration of self-disclosure after traumatic brain injury. Ph.D. Thesis. Birmingham, UK: University of Birmingham. Available at: http://etheses.bham.ac.uk/3080/1/Hagger11PhD.pdf.

Halkier, B. (2010). Focus groups as social enactments: Integrating interaction and content in the analysis of focus group data. *Qualitative Research*, 10(1), 71–89.

Haslam, C., Holme, A., Haslam, S. A., Iver, A., Jetten, J., & Williams, W. H. (2008). Maintaining group memberships: Social identity continuity predicts well-being after stroke. *Neuropsychological Rehabilitation*, 8(5–6), 671–691.

Hibbard, M. R., Cantor, J., Charatz, H., Rosenthal, R., Ashman, T., Gundersen, N., … Gartner, A. (2002). Peer support in the community: Initial findings of a mentoring program for individuals with traumatic brain injury and their families. *Journal of Head Trauma Rehabilitation*, 17(2), 112–131.

Iverson, G. L., Lange, R. T., Brooks, B. L., & Rennison, V. L. A. (2010). "Good old days" bias following mild traumatic brain injury. *The Clinical Neuropsychologist*, 24(1), 17–37.

Jones, J. M., Williams, W. H., Jetten, J., Haslam, S. A., Harris, A., & Gleibs, I. H. (2012). The role of psychological symptoms and social group memberships in the development of post-traumatic stress after traumatic injury. *British Journal of Health Psychology*, 17(4), 798–811.

Karpatschof, B. (2007). Bringing quality and meaning to quantitative data, bringing quantitative evidence to qualitative observation. *Nordic Psychology*, 59(3), 191–209.

Lexell, E. M., Alkhed, A. K., & Olsson, K. (2013). The group rehabilitation helped me adjust to a new life: Experiences shared by persons with an acquired brain injury. *Brain Injury*, 27(5), 529–537.

McLean, A. M., Jarus, T., Hubley, A. M., & Jongbloed, L. (2012). Differences in social participation between individuals who do and do not attend brain injury drop-in centres: A preliminary study. *Brain Injury*, 26(1), 83–94.

Morton, M. V. & Wehman, P. (1995). Psychosocial and emotional sequelae of individuals with traumatic brain injury: A literature review and recommendations. *Brain Injury*, 9(1), 81–92.

Mozo-Dutton, L., Simpson, J., & Boot, J. (2012). MS and me: Exploring the impact of multiple sclerosis on perceptions of self. *Disability and Rehabilitation*, 34(14), 1208–1217.

Nochi, M. (1997). Dealing with the "Void": Traumatic brain injury as a story. *Disability & Society*, 12(4), 533–555.

Nochi, M. (1998). Struggling with the labeled self: People with traumatic brain injuries in social settings. *Qualitative Health Research*, 8(5), 665–681.

Olsen, L. & Bonfils, I. S. (2013). Valg af handicapbegreber gør stor forskel, også i forskning. In I. S. Bonfils, B. Kirkebæk, L. Olsen & S. Tetler (Eds.), *Handicapforståelser – mellem teori, erfaring og virkelighed* (pp. 109–118). Copenhagen, Denmark: Akademisk forlag.

Rasmussen, P. S., Navne, L. E., Fulgsang, T., & Kruse, M. (2014). *Helhed for hjerneskadede*. Copenhagen, Denmark: KORA.

Salas, C. E., Casassus, M., Rowlands, L., & Pimm, S. (2018). Relating through sameness: A qualitative study of friendship and social isolation in chronic traumatic brain injury. *Neuropsychological Rehabilitation*, 28(7), 1161–1178.

Schwartzberg, S. L. (1994). Helping factors in a peer-developed support group for persons with head-injury, Part 1: Participant observer perspective. *American Journal of Occupational Therapy*, 48(4), 297–304.

Shadden, B. B. & Agan, J. P. (2004). Renegotiation of identity: The social context of aphasia support groups. *Topics in Language Disorders*, 24(3), 174–186.

Wiuff, M. B., Navne, L. E., & Olesen, E. O. (2010). *Rehabilitering på borgernes premisser*. Copenhagen, Denmark: DSI.

Part III

Future perspectives on neurorehabilitation

The following chapters unfold ideas and perspectives for future directions in ABI rehabilitation.

12 Psychological rehabilitation

Looking at the results of my research, in general and in the light of the bio–psycho–social model, I find that the psychological aspects of the model especially remain unaddressed in rehabilitation practice. Offering psychological support in the long-term perspective is necessary to distinguish and support those who may develop signs of emotional distress post-injury. Considering the acquired brain injury (ABI) survivors' and relatives' accounts, not only service transitions but also life and identity transitions after ABI must be supported. The results of my research indicate that life and identity transitions require more attention. Furthermore, the results revealed that there is still a main focus on physical rehabilitation. Moreover, rehabilitation services do not empower persons with ABI sufficiently during this transition to enable them to face everyday life again. Persons with ABI were not offered support in coping with their emotional distress, e.g. identity problems. The paradigmatic change in brain injury rehabilitation, which began in the late 1980s, includes a change in focus from purely physical aspects to a broader picture including the psychosocial consequences of brain injury. Therefore, rehabilitation requires interdisciplinary collaboration and coordination between professionals, persons with ABI, and their relatives, in order to address the physical, psychological, and social needs of the client. This is also noted and highlighted by the UN in the Convention of Rights for People with Disabilities (CRPD). According to the UN CRPD, rehabilitation efforts must begin at "the earliest possible stage," and be "based on the multidisciplinary assessment of individual needs and strengths" (UN, 2006). However, as seen, coordination does not ensure an encompassing and coherent approach (Glintborg & Hansen, 2016). Psychologists are present in the first phase of the rehabilitation process. However, they are represented in the form of neuropsychological praxis that mainly involves testing. Looking abroad, I find that rehabilitation psychology has been growing as a field, especially in the US, though rather less in Europe. Rehabilitation psychology is defined as:

> A specialty area within psychology that focuses on the study and application of psychological knowledge and skills on behalf of individuals with disabilities and chronic health conditions in order to maximize health and welfare, independence and choice, functional abilities, and social role participation across the lifespan.
> (Division 22 of the American Psychological Association, n.d.)

Rehabilitation psychological services not only address a person's psychosocial needs, but also those of their family. Family interventions must be conducted so as to meet the changing needs of ABI survivors and their relatives.

Accounts from persons with ABI and their relatives indicate a gap in the services being provided, particularly a lack of psychological rehabilitation (Glintborg & Hansen, 2016). This approach to the issue of rehabilitation might solve some of the current problems in addressing the psychosocial consequences of ABI. Furthermore, it would enhance progress toward the ambition of a coherent and comprehensive rehabilitation approach based on the bio–psycho–social model.

The psychological trauma

When you acquire a brain injury, it is not only a neurological trauma, but also, to a large extent, a psychological trauma. ABI is a life-changing event. An individual not only loses bodily functions, but also social and relational positions (work, network, family, etc.). Entering into the rehabilitation system can be a second psychological trauma. Interactions with professionals in the form of improper practices, childish assertion, removal of hope, and social inequality in the treatment, as illustrated in this book, can also be traumatizing. Several years of traumatization can develop into severe disorders such as depression, anxiety, and a general distrust of the system. This can result in the use of evasive coping strategies, which again can be misinterpreted as lack of motivation.

There is a need to rethink notions like lack of insight and lack of motivation. Is it always lack of insight? Or could it be a way of dealing with things that are, as yet, too difficult to deal with (i.e. a defense mechanism)? The recognition of our shared humanity is crucial. Instead of dehumanizing and pathologizing ABI survivors, normalization could be an important aspect to consider further, as it suggests a basic mutuality in the experience of suffering. As long as there is so much stigma attached to ABI, acceptance of being a person with ABI can be difficult and extremely shameful. We need to validate this fact much more in rehabilitation and maybe rethink why professionals believe insight to be so important. Could it not serve a protective function when patients challenge ABI? Maybe we should start validating and normalizing accounts from ABI survivors as good practice instead of using methods involving confrontation and correction of reality, since this traditional practice seems to fail in its purpose of leading to greater insight into and acceptance of difficulties and thence to a greater motivation to work with these difficulties. On the contrary, confrontations can lead to participants either giving up and thus losing motivation or to their developing mental resistance (Rollnick, Miller, & Butler, 2013). Therefore, we might need to rethink the concept of insight. Furthermore, we should start reflecting on what happens to an individual's identity when they are met with disbelief in what they are saying. We should create more *sameness* with ABI survivors, not difference. This approach contrasts with a more traditional and distanced professional/expert vs. client approach, and underscores the need for a new knowledge regime in neurorehabilitation.

The value of relating to other survivors

Our study on peer support groups (Chapter 11) indicates that support groups can play a very important role in the process of identity (re) construction after ABI. The peer support group facilitates the difficult and lengthy adaptation process and enhances a given person's agency toward themselves and others. The mechanisms through which this happens include recognition and understanding from the peers' perspectives and a (re)definition of old and new values. With this in mind, we should consider the possibility of embedding participation in a peer support group into the current rehabilitation approaches.

On the other hand, support peer groups may not always be sufficient when dealing with the chronic consequences of a disease. The presented data also contain indications that, for example, psychological assistance is in high demand, yet is rare – both regarding the injured persons and their relatives. As Jette from SG1 states: "… *the psychologist services, I think, that should be a must, I mean one should not even have to ask, because that is what we all need so badly.*" That participants in SG2 did not express the same need for a psychologist may be due to the much higher chronicity and thereby a greater degree of transition to post-injury life. Furthermore, the analysis also showed that groups can function quite differently depending on the configuration of their participants and their individual character-istics. It is fair to say that peer support may work best if the group participants are relatively homogenous. Additionally, the group may not always enable the articulation of each participant's views, and may be restrictive regarding which discourses are welcome and validated. For instance, in SG2 negative narratives were apparently undesirable. Other dominant discourses may keep the individual participant in a passive role for a longer period than they would otherwise choose, in particular, when there is a high identification of the individual with the group. It is therefore worth considering whether a presence of a psychologist at certain times (e.g. in the beginning or according to a fixed schedule) would strengthen the respondents' abilities to see beyond the limitations of their illnesses and result in more adequate discourses for identity (re)construction. For instance, Couchman et al. showed that a therapist-led group with peers and their relatives can have a positive effect on the reconciliation between the old and current self-image and lead to the development of a new form of normality. Moreover, it also promoted a common framework for understanding the situation and the experiences all affected persons go through. This in turn enhanced the construction of adaptive discourses that were available both in and outside the support group. However, as pointed out by the authors, the presence of relatives may have meant that there was less space for emotional topics, as these were harder to address in a big group (Couchman, McMahon, Kelly, & Ponsford, 2014).

Moreover, a psychologist would also be helpful in a situation where the group fails to promote agency. In such a scenario, the psychologist would be able to uncover the resources that are already present in the group and direct them toward a construction of more adaptive discourses. A focus on agency in the support group can also help its participants to be more strategic regarding the appli-cation of self-narratives and thereby assist each other in a con-struction of a coherent self-image before and after ABI (Glintborg & Krogh, 2015). Finally, research also shows that psychological interventions (such as cognitive behavioral therapy) are efficient at reducing depression and anxiety associated with chronic neurologi-cal conditions, for example (Uccelli, Mohr, Battaglia, Zagami, & Mohr, 2004; Waldron, Casserly, & O'Sullivan, 2013). However, another factor to be considered is whether the presence of a pro-fessional may inhibit some of the positive processes that arise in the informal settings of peer context.

Personal competencies in professionals – the way of being that makes a difference

Many of the participants in my research remembered a professional who had had a lasting, positive impact on them. But what is it about this kind of person that leaves a long-term positive impression? Maybe this person "believed in me when I was going through a tough time." Or perhaps that person "saw something in me that no one else could see."

Considering the lifelong impact such a person can have, they usually tend to be humble. These professionals seem more interested in the success of others than in their own reputation or standing. They are curious about their clients. They show genuine interest in clients and treat them with respect and equality. They believe that their clients have enormous potential. These qualities, or ways of interacting with others, form the basis for what Carl Rogers (1980) termed a "way of being."

What seems to make the crucial difference in rehabilitation effectiveness is "the way of being" of the professional. The importance of an emotional connection and the complete understanding of the other person was underpinned by Carl Rogers, founder of humanistic psychology, years ago, but have we forgotten this valuable insight into relationships? Within neurorehabilitation most education for professionals focuses on how we can increase our neurological knowledge of brain injuries. Rarely are there courses focusing on the relationship between the professionals and the adults with ABI. Therefore, this last part of the book will look further into the concept of ways of being, and revitalize some of Rogers's valuable insights when humans are dealing with humans.

We are all individuals who are dealing with people. In the article "What Understanding and Acceptance Mean to Me," Carl Rogers underpins what he has learned about understanding and empathy. He makes four statements regarding this:

1. It does not help to act as though I were something that I am not

> For instance, it does not help to behave in an understanding way when, actually, you are trying to manipulate the other person, not understand him or her. Or to appear calm and pleasant, when in fact you are angry and critical. What Rogers is saying is that it is not helpful to maintain a façade, to act in one way on the surface while experiencing something different underneath. It does not make you helpful in building up relationships with other individuals.

2. To be acceptant of my self

What am I feeling in any giving moment? It is important to register that I am angry, that I feel rejection toward this person, or that I am uninterested. We need to listen to the feelings that clients evoke in us. When we use ourselves as the most important tool in helping others, we also need to look into our diverse attitudes and listen to our feelings. In this way professionals can become better at letting the clients be what they are. The curious paradox is that once we learn to accept, then we seem able to change. Another result that grows out of self-acceptance is that relationships become real, not instrumental. You are not necessarily the expert who knows everything, demonstrating that this expertise can make a change happen in the client.

3. To really understand the other person

According to Rogers, it is necessary to *permit* oneself to understand another person. Our first reaction to statements we hear from other people is an immediate evaluation, or judgement, rather than an understanding of it. When a client expresses some feelings or attitudes our tendency is, almost immediately, to evaluate it, i.e. as good, right or wrong, incorrect, etc. Very rarely do we permit ourselves to understand precisely the meaning of this statement to the other person. The understanding of a professional permits the individual to change. i.e. if you fully understand the feelings of the other person, this can enable them to accept those feelings in themselves.

4. When I can accept another person

Can I accept a client when they view life and psychological problems differently? Can I permit a client to feel hostile toward me? Can I accept a client's anger? An increasingly common pattern in our culture is that every other person must think, feel, and believe the same as I do. The importance of seeing another person choose his or her own way is one of the most priceless potentialities in life. Thus, *"When I can be myself, when I accept myself, then it is possible for me to understand others and accept others."*

(Rogers, 1995, p. 19)

A final teaching of Rogers is that persons seeking help basically have positive directions. In contact with adults in therapy, he experienced this to be true, even in those whose troubles were most disturbing. When you as a professional can sensitively understand the feelings expressed by the other, when you are able to accept them as separate persons in their own right, then they move in positive, constructive ways toward self-actualization. When an individual feels fully understood and accepted, he or she tends to drop the false front that they have been meeting life, and the more they move forward.

References

Couchman, G., McMahon, G., Kelly, A., & Ponsford, J. (2014). A new kind of normal: Qualitative accounts of Multifamily Group Therapy for acquired brain injury. *Neuropsychological Rehabilitation*, 24(6), 809–832.

Division 22 of the American Psychological Association. (n.d.) What is Rehab Psych?: Introduction. Available at: www.div22.org/what-is-rehab-psych/.

Glintborg, C. & Hansen, T. G. (2016). Bio–psycho–social effects of a coordinated neurorehabilitation programme: A naturalistic mixed methods study. *NeuroRehabilitation*, 38(2), 99–113.

Glintborg, C. & Krogh, L. (2015). Identitets (re)konstruktioner hos mennesker med en erhvervet hjerneskade. Et casestudie af selv-narrativer og diskurser på hjerneskadeområdet [Identity (re)constructions in survivors of brain injury. A case study of self-narratives and discourses after brain injury]. *Globe: A Journal on Language, Communications and Culture*, 1, 93–106.

Rollnick, S., Miller, W. R., & Butler, C. C. (2013). *Motivationssamtalen i sundhedssektoren*. Copenhagen, Denmark: Hans Reitzels Forlag.

Rogers, C. R. (1980). *A way of being*. Boston, MA: Houghton Mifflin.

Rogers, C. R. (1995). What understanding and acceptance mean to me. *Journal of Humanistic Psychology*, 35(4), 7–22.

Uccelli, M. M., Mohr, L. M., Battaglia, M. A., Zagami, P., & Mohr, D. C. (2004). Peer support groups in multiple sclerosis: Current effectiveness and future directions. *Multiple Sclerosis*, 10(1), 80–84.

United Nations (2006). *Convention on the rights of persons with disabilities*. Available at: www.un.org/development/desa/disabilities/convention-on-the-rights-of-persons-with-disabilities/convention-on-the-rights-of-persons-with-disabilities-2.html.

Waldron, B., Casserly, L. M., & O'Sullivan, C. (2013). Cognitive behavioural therapy for depression and anxiety in adults with acquired brain injury: What works for whom? *Neuropsychological Rehabilitation*, 23(1), 64–101.

13 Concluding reflections

Over the last 30 years, rehabilitation services have been dominated by the health care professionals who provide it. This predominance of professional values in training, practice, and research has led to a circular system that discourages the contribution of adults with acquired brain injury (ABI) and their close relatives. There has been a growing recognition of the importance of social reality. Social reality is constructed through shared talks and in rehabilitation two types are possible: (1) that of the professional, and (2) that of the adults with ABI. Research has shown that there is still a gap between professional and personal understanding and experience (Doolittle, 1992; Cott, 2004) For instance, for professionals, the physical recovery following ABI can be seen as the focus of intervention, whereas research has found that, although the clients themselves see physical improvement as important, the focus for them was their return to a pre-ABI life. This gap between professional and personal realities reduces the effectiveness of rehabilitation. Thus, the experience of ABI goes far beyond living with the loss of functional ability.

As demonstrated in this book, ABI is still predominantly seen in terms of deficits and functional loss, and the focus is on the physical body and tasks the individual can no longer perform. Thus, ABI is associated with limitations, problems, and difficulties that are not usually experienced by an able person. This may support the negative view that adults with ABI are in some ways "less than" other people. This loss discourse is more characteristic among health care professionals than among adults with ABI themselves (Alaszewski, Alaszewski, & Potter, 2004).

Currently, the emotional consequences following ABI are poorly understood. Mood change and distress have been ascribed to the brain injury itself (Kadojic et al., 2005). Psychological and emotional support has been thought to be outside of the expertise of most health care professionals. Since, clinical psychologists are in short supply, this limits the potential of rehabilitation to resolve emotional issues.

Over the last 30 years, researchers have placed increased emphasis on the meaning and experience of disabling illness and on negotiation of self and identity in everyday life (Williams, 1999). Psychological research by Sarbin (1986), and as presented in this book, has explored the social processes that have an impact on identity and a sense of self. There has been an increasing recognition of the importance of narrative approaches in medicine in general (Charon, 2001; Connelly, 2005) and specifically in rehabilitation (Clark, 1993; Faircloth, Rittman, Boylstein, Young, & van Puymbroeck, 2004).

Narrative analysis can be a potentially powerful approach in its ability to capture transitions within identity and co-creation of positions for ABI survivors and their close relatives. Narrative inquiry amplifies voices that may have otherwise remained silent. In this book, it has been illustrated that the individual with ABI, and their close relatives, are *not* liberated from categorical terms (e.g., normal, disabled, brain damaged, etc.). In the current knowledge regime in neurorehabilitation there are certain accessible discourses, however these discourses mainly draw on a medical understanding of ABI. Narratives from ABI survivors and relatives exemplify how a medical gaze comes to prevail, and how difficult it can be to make sense of emotional distress when diagnostic language dominates.

References

Alaszewski, A., Alaszewski, H., & Potter, J. (2004). The bereavement model, stroke and rehabilitation: A critical analysis of the use of a psychological model in professional practice. *Disability & Rehabilitation*, 26(18), 1067–1078.

Charon, R. (2001). Narrative medicine. *Journal American Medical Association*, 286(15), 1897–1902.

Clark, F. (1993). Occupation embedded in a real-life: Interweaving occupational science and occupational therapy. Eleanor Clarke Slagle lecture. *American Journal of Occupational Therapy*, 47(12), 1067–1078.

Connelly, J. E. (2005). Narrative possibilities: Using mindfulness in clinical practice. *Perspectives in Biology and Medicine*, 48(1), 84–94.

Cott, C. A. (2004). Client-centred rehabilitation: Client perspectives. *Disability & Rehabilitation*, 26(24), 1411–1422.

Doolittle, N. (1992). The experience of recovery following lacunar stroke. *Rehabilitation Nursing*, 17(3), 122–125.

Faircloth, C. A., Rittman, M., Boylstein, C., Young, M.E., & van Puymbroeck, M. (2004). Energizing the ordinary: Biographical work and the future in stroke recovery narratives. *Journal of Aging Studies*, 18(4), 399–413.

Kadojic, D., Vladetic, M., Candrlic, M., Kadojic, M., Dikanovic, M., & Trkanjec, Z. (2005). Frequency and characteristics of emotional disorders in patients after ischemic stroke. *The European Journal of Psychiatry*, 19(2), 88–95.

Sarbin, T. (1986). *Narrative psychology. The storied nature of human conduct.* New York: Praeger.

Williams, S. J. (1999). Is anybody there? Critical realism, chronic illness and the disability debate. *Sociology of Health & Illness*, 21(6), 797–819.

Index

Printed in the United States
by Baker & Taylor Publisher Services

Printed in the United States
by Baker & Taylor Publisher Services